Praise for *What Do I Need to KNOW?*

"Rev. Rita's personal life experiences make the spiritual principles of this book easy to comprehend and apply to my own life. I will read these blogs again and again as each one speaks to me anew each time I randomly open to a page."

SUE BUCKLEY

"Rev. Rita's beautifully written inspirational words always seem to feed and nourish my soul at the right time."

JOAN MORGAN

"Rev. Rita has a precious gift of sharing her everyday experiences and turning them into spiritual blessings. Her deep insights have added so much to enriching my spiritual journey."

SHARI TEAL

What Do I Need to KNOW?

101 THOUGHTS THAT CHANGED MY LIFE

Rev. Rita Andriello-Feren

Cover and Interior design by Jonathan Zenz
Published in the United States of America

For Patrick Feren who taught me unconditional love.

Table of Contents

FOREWORD

It was Christmas of 2006 when a bright, beautiful, charismatic woman entered the doors of the NoHo Arts Center for New Thought in Southern California and made her presence known. Her energy was vibrant and her eyes shone a Truth that was palpable. She knew who she was, and she instantly showed you just how valuable you were in her eyes. She had a thirst for life and an unabashed enthusiasm for living that was and is to this day contagious. This began a lifelong friendship that, to this day, is one of the greatest blessings in my life. This was/is Rev. Rita Andriello.

The book you have before you is an insight into the heart, soul, and consciousness of one of the most spiritually evolved beings I have been blessed to both teach and learn from. Rev. Rita's newest book, What Do I Need to KNOW, is a tool that will help you understand who you are and what is yours to do in any given scenario. Her simple and yet profound understanding of life is a guiding light in a world of too many dark corners, written by a person who has traveled to the depths and heights of what it means to be a Divine Human Being.

Like me, Rita grew up Catholic. She knows her way around scripture and has an uncanny sense of Spiritual Logic. She has studied the World Religions and has embraced all philosophies that teach love, acceptance, diversity, and creativity. In this book, Rev. Rita shows the reader a way to allow the Divine to speak to each of us in terms of common experiences and to know that, no matter what is going on, you are bigger than any situation that may come your way. Knowing who you are is a fundamental necessity in a world of conflicting truths and shifting tides. This book gives each of us the common sense and yet inspired way of looking at the things that sometimes perplex us in our everyday lives.

At the end of each post there is an affirmation that serves as a spiritual balm for whatever issue you might be experiencing. Use these quotes as a way to navigate the journey of your life. By the end of this book, you will have accumulated a wealth of words and phrases, ideas and understandings that will expand your heart, soothe your mind, and stimulate your creative soul. I am so grateful to have been and continue to be a part of this amazing woman's life. Her heart knows no bounds as she continues to teach us all what it means to be Spiritual Beings living in this most exquisite Universe.

Dr. James Mellon
Founding Spiritual Director
Global Truth Center

INTRODUCTION

IN 2010, A DEAR FRIEND OF MINE was diagnosed with cancer. I was inspired to ask him if I could write a Spiritual Mind Treatment for him every day. A Spiritual Mind Treatment is an affirmative prayer that moves energy in the direction of our desired intention. My friend was grateful for my offer and willingly accepted it. Thus started my blog writing.

Several months later he went through his healing and I discontinued sending him my Treatments. However, I couldn't stop writing and my daily Treatments turned into daily blogging. My writing habit was so ingrained in me that, no matter my schedule, I would get up as early as necessary to make sure I kept my date with my written word. I never missed a day for over six years.

My readers would often tell me they printed out my blogs and kept them to refer to throughout their day. I was told by many how much they appreciated my words and how those words rang true for them at just the right time. "*Why don't you put them into a book?*" I was often asked. I hesitated for a long time. Finally, I gave in. Why is it called *What Do I Need to Know*? Well, when I woke up each morning that is the question I asked of my Higher Self. Then, I'd put my fingers on the keys and begin writing.

I present the blogs in this book in no particular order. I invite you to ask your Higher Self, "*What do I need to know?*" and then turn to any page. Follow your intuition. If you feel like reading these blogs in order, go for it. If you feel like skipping around or reading the whole book in one sitting, go for it. You know best for yourself and you are always at choice.

In order for the blogs have some context, I'd like to acquaint you with my belief system. I have come to believe in one all-inclusive Power. I call it by many names: Infinite Intelligence, Source Energy, the Unified Field, and God. God to me is a Presence *and* a Principle.

What is this Principle? There is only One Power, everywhere present. That means it is in everything. This Power is Love and nothing but Love. This Power is unlimited. It gives of itself continuously, forever eternal. It has no beginning and no end. It cannot help but express itself and take on form. This Power is what I am, aback of my form. It is my eternal Consciousness forever-expanding. It is the same for you. We are Eternal expanding Spirit.

This All-Inclusive Power operates through Its Law; the Law of Cause and Effect. This Law receives the impress of our thought and acts upon it. Whatever we believe consistently with enough feeling out-pictures as our experience. I use the word "experience" to differentiate between what we are (God, Love) and how we use the Law. The Law is a natural force that attracts and repels. The more we are aligned with our unlimited God Nature, the more unlimited our experience, because the Law of our being can only be to us what we know and accept it to be. Simply put, it reacts to us at the level of our belief.

Because we are always at choice, we get to decide on our experience. We are each a spontaneous individualization of God at choice in every moment. We are even choosing by not choosing. We are always using the Law consciously or unconsciously. My journey is to use it consciously.

I do not believe in anything as "just happening to me." I do not believe in happenstance or a disorderly Universe. I do not believe the stars govern me. I do not believe that someone else can do something to my mind unless I let them. If I believe holding a crystal will help me, it will because *it is done unto me as I believe.* If something occurs in my experience, I believe I am responsible for it being there and, with this responsibility, I can change the course of my life in a moment by choosing differently.

Dr. Ernest Holmes, Founder of the Science of Mind and Spirit, is someone I quote numerous times throughout this book. He wrote in all caps, in the *Science of Mind*, "*WE MAY CHANGE THE TREND OF CAUSATION WHICH HAS BEEN SET IN MOTION AT ANY TIME WE DECIDE TO DO SO.*"

I prefer to live my life this way. I like taking 100% responsibility for my experiences. However, I understand that other people think differently and are also free and have volition or choice. Therefore, I condemn nothing and do my best to love each person for exactly where they are in their lives.

What about Heaven? It's not a place we go. Although we take a different path, we are already in Heaven because Heaven is a state of mind. Heaven is always right where we are to the degree that we are aware of it. So, we can travel as far away as we want in mind, but the hearth of Love is always here in the heart. The story of the Prodigal Son as told by the Master Jesus explains this in a powerful parable. It's worth a read and Ernest Holmes gives a simple explanation for this parable (Holmes 1926, *Science of Mind*, 460).

I believe in Love, not in the fairy tale sense of the word (although I like fairy tales), but in the sense that Love is what we are. We have always been Love and always will be Love. It is not something we need to get or possess. It is our natural state of being. And the second half is that Love operates through an impersonal Law that is always saying yes to us. We lead the way and the Law makes our way possible. In quantum science it is said, our intention sends a signal out into the Unified Field of Energy, and our feeling brings it back to us. It's Law.As you read these blogs, I hope they will shed a little light on how I have applied this Principle to my life. Remember, until we apply the Principle and prove it to ourselves, we do not truly know it. I invite you to keep an open mind and read on. I am knowing that my writing will assist you during these amazing and challenging times in which we live. Thank you for taking the journey. You are here because you are meant to be. The Universe (You) doesn't make mistakes.

1

All Things Are Possible!

Jesus looked at them and said, "*With man this is impossible, but with God all things are possible*" (Matthew 19:26).

I don't know what your belief system is, but I believe that the Consciousness of the man named Jesus was the Consciousness of the Christ and that Consciousness knows its true identity and knows its Divinity. I believe that Consciousness is within each one of us.

I have no idea whether Jesus came here fully evolved in that Consciousness or whether he became illumined within his time on this planet. It doesn't really matter to me. What matters is what I can glean from his teachings and words and parables and ideas.

In the statement above, I am given a very important Truth. When I set about to do something and my finite mind thinks it is impossible, it is impossible. However, when I know that with the Infinite, all things are possible, then so it is.

Ernest Holmes, mystic and founder of Science of Mind and Spirit, used to state that, "*There is a Power for Good in the Universe greater than we are and we can use it.*" He was talking about the Law of our being, the great Universal Law of Cause and Effect. We can use it, not because it is outside of ourselves, but because it is within each and every one of us. It is Infinite, and with this Infinite Intelligence that serves us, we can always know that all things are possible. We must get out of the way of outlining our outcomes or puzzling on how they will happen, and trust that they have already happened.

Today, I am thinking of many things that I have to accomplish this year, trips I want to take, projects to complete, many of which can seem like insurmountable tasks. However, if I can truly surrender them to the Law of my being, that Infinite Power, if I can let go of my own inability to get them done with my finite means, everything is possible.

Does this mean I do not do anything and turn on my favorite TV show or go to sleep? Well, sometimes it does. However, it also means that I stop worrying long enough to allow Divine Wisdom, my intuition, to take over and lead the way. The doors open, the people appear, and money comes from unpredictable sources. If I am quiet for long enough and can cease my lamenting and complaining, I will hear and see the way.

Something happened recently that brings this point home. We were working on the budget for our Spiritual Center. We were several thousand dollars in the red. Of course, we didn't want to present this budget to our congregation. How could we bring it into the black? We were at our Board Meeting telling our Board how we had just today gotten news of a donor who wanted to increase his donation by a certain amount. One of the Board members said, "*Do you realize that is the exact amount of this deficit!*" It was and we hadn't even realized it until that moment.

"*With man this is impossible, but with God all things are possible.*"

What can you turn over to God today?

Affirmation:
I am living in the unlimited field of possibilities.

2

You Can't Outgive God

"*You can't outgive God*." This philosophy was shared with me by my mentor, Dr. James Mellon. Every time we'd be working on the finances of his Spiritual Center or having some specific financial dilemma, he'd say, "*You can't outgive God*." He'd then make the payment, give the donation, pick up the tab, or write the check for whatever it was. Everything always worked out and flowed.

This is a powerful statement if truly understood and felt. For me, it says that no matter what financial issue is in front of me, I am safe to move forward and take care of it. And something as simple as leaving a tip that is a little more generous than I might have left becomes a joy. If "*I can't outgive God*," it means that there is always more where that came from—more money, more resources, more love, more time, more energy, more of everything.

How does it work? It's not just words; it is the feeling and understanding and faith behind the words. "*You can't outgive God*" is not a plea to or recognition of an outside Deity. It is trusting in the inner Source of my being. It is knowing that the more I give, the more I have. It is un-kinking the hose of prosperity and increasing its flow.

It is not always easy and sometimes I notice that I pause, take a gulp, and then let that breath go. I mentally open my hand to give and receive.

"*You can't outgive God, Rita*" is a powerful mantra for me. It relieves tension surrounding money. It increases my faith. It is a point of surrender to the Source of my being.

Anne Frank wrote, "*No one has ever become poor by giving.*" Wow! What a concept! Think about it. It's really true.

Affirmation:
I can't outgive God.

3

It's Always the Season
for Nonviolence

It is another Season for Nonviolence. If you do not know what it is, the Season of Nonviolence is 64 days put aside every year between January 30 (the assassination of Gandhi) and April 4 (the assassination of Martin Luther King, Jr.) devoted to the practice of nonviolence. The Season was established by Arun Gandhi, Mahatma Gandhi's grandson, in 1998 as a yearly event celebrating the philosophies and lives of Mohandas Gandhi and Martin Luther King, Jr.

I am thinking of this particularly wonderful, inspiring idea. I remember a Spiritual Center I used to attend that celebrated this tradition every year. There is a calendar that has a principle of nonviolence to practice each day. On each Sunday, while reading a short quote, this Center lit a candle for each of the principles that week.

It was a beautiful tradition. However, we must get beyond words and traditions and rituals. I am all for them, but if they do not bring us to action, what good are they? Many people have tried to change the world through their words and those great people put those words into action—Gandhi, Martin Luther King, Jr., Jesus, and others. There are many people we know of who are less famous, including ourselves, who have put our words into action.

We might ask, "Why hasn't the world changed? Why are we still at war? Why is there poverty?" Remember the song, Where Have All the Flowers Gone? Well, "When will we ever learn?"

Could it be that we follow these great Way showers while they are here and then their messages begin to dissipate when they leave? We fail to do it on our own, to lead ourselves. I believe it is because we are not getting the principles of nonviolence on an individual level. The individual must heal himself before the world will heal.

I heard the distressing news yesterday that someone I knew briefly just hung himself. What would bring someone to end his or her own life? Why didn't I know so I could help? We might blame it on chemical imbalances, depression, mental illness, etc. We throw our hands up in the air and ask, "Why didn't he get help? Why wasn't he helped?"

First of all, we do not know the answer. How far back can I step to measure another person's life or his or her decisions? I don't know. However, I do know this. I do know that unconditional love is the answer to everything. I know that wherever this person is right now, I can know that he is surrounded by, infused with, and supported by unconditional love.

We cannot change the world. We can only change ourselves. We cannot expect other people to act the way we want them to act. We can only be examples of Love. We can live our lives fully and filled with love. We can take care of our own lives and reach out from within to assist others.

We do not need to wait for the Season of Nonviolence to make a difference. We do not need to light a candle or recite a poem. We can go into our own closets and return there over and over until we are transformed enough to live from the space of unconditional love.

I do not want to change the world. I want to change myself.

I invite us all to forgive ourselves, appreciate ourselves, and love ourselves by remembering who we are.

I am stuck on the words of Martin Luther King, Jr. *"Our goal is to create a beloved community and this will require a qualitative change in our souls and a quantitative change in our lives."*

We each must go through this change.

Affirmation:
I am unconditional love.

4

Calling All Successful People

"The planet does not need more successful people. The planet desperately needs more peacemakers, healers, restorers, storytellers and lovers of all kinds" (His Holiness the 14th Dalai Lama).

Do you agree with the Dalai Lama? I both agree and disagree. When he says the world does not need more successful people, I would disagree. Perhaps, we do not need people striving for success as their only goal. A person just striving for success alone could end up giving up a lot along the way.

However, we do need more successful people. What I define as success is the outcome of a well-lived life. Success is the outcome of living our true selves, our passions. Success is the outcome of being at one with ourselves and others. Successful people in the truest sense are people who reveal the glory of the Divine. I would say that the Dalai Lama is a successful person. He lives his Truth. He lives by example. He inspires us all to be better, to love more.

So, yes, the world needs more successful people. Not those striving to be successful, but those striving to live life to the fullest, to be happy, to serve, to love.

He goes on to say that the planet *"desperately needs more peacemakers, healers, restorers, storytellers and lovers of all kinds."* Yes, these are successful people. Where do you fit in?

I believe I am working on being all these things. I strive to be peaceful in my life. I want to heal with my presence. What is a restorer? My dad used to love to restore old furniture and make it beautiful. We can always restore our lives, taking what has gotten off track and bringing it back to its wholeness. We should never give up on this idea. We can always restore what seems broken or lost. Right under the surface is the true nature of whatever it is - the spiritual prototype that is perfect.

And what about storytellers? Yes, our stories are important. We should share them, not to lament about them, but to be inspiring. We can share where we have been and where we are now. I love a good inspiring story. I love to share my own inspiration.

Lastly, the Dalai Lama says we need *"lovers of all kinds."* What does it mean to be a lover? I don't think he is talking about making love in a sexual sense. Although that's certainly good. I believe he means lovers of life and others.

The Dalai Lama is always smiling. There is a reason for that. It is a genuine, contagious smile. It comes from the deep love that emanates from within him. He truly sees the good in life and lives from that place. If I am to be a lover, I must love life, and live life like I love it.

We are so blessed to live right now at this time. We get to be all these things. We get to be restorers every day. We get to be storytellers and share our rich pasts to inspire. We get to be healers by being the presence of wholeness by seeing it in others wherever we go. We get to be peacemakers, beginning within ourselves, and emanating that peace out into our lives and the world. We get to be lovers of life.

What a beautiful challenge that the Dalai Lama has given us

and one that is definitely achievable. We are all Dalai Lamas blooming right now. As Mother Teresa said, *"Bloom (grow) where you are planted."*

Are you blooming? Yes, you are!

Affirmation:
I am blooming where I am planted.

5

We Have the Power to Begin Again

Thomas Paine, who influenced the American Revolution and paved the way for the Declaration of Independence wrote, "*We have it in our power to begin the world over again.*"

Ernest Holmes once wrote, "*ANYTHING YOU CAN DREAM OF is not too great for you to undertake, if it hurts no one and brings happiness and good into your life.*"

We are working with, through and as an unlimited Power that created the Cosmos. It is our life right now. The here and now is where this Power is. We have It in our Power. The more we become aware of It, the more It becomes aware of us.

This is the time for us to step into our Power and use it for Good. I believe that the most important thing that we can do right now is to live our lives to the fullest. All those dreams we had tucked away and were waiting to accomplish need to be lived now. If each person were living their true life, the one that gives them joy, the one led by passion, we would do more to uplift the planet.

The day of making excuses for ourselves can be put away. We have turned our lives over to others' opinions for too long. We have let apathy and hopelessness create a world led by a few. If we don't have vision, we become part of someone else's vision.

We do have a voice. We do have the Power. It is Spiritual Power. It is unlimited. It is our ability to make choices and visualize and speak those choices into Universal Law and then act accordingly.

We cannot change others but we can change ourselves. We can change our thinking from hopelessness and self-absorption in misery to living our life to the fullest expression of love. We can begin this right where we are, with who is right next to us, and then take it out into the world step by step.

We can stop hiding from ourselves and our True Nature. It is okay to have confidence in our beauty. It is okay to be great. What is greater than a Divine idea in the mind of God? That is what I am. That is what you are.

"*Ask, and it shall be given*" (Matthew 7:7). We have to announce what we want. We have to act as if we already have it. We have to direct our minds by love and nothing else. We must love, beginning with the self, and reflect that self out into our world.

I am grateful for the Life that lives and breathes through me. I am grateful for the blessings of awakening in this changing world and knowing that I am responsible for how I live in it. I am a projector of life, of love, and of unity. I will do my best to remember this.

I agree with Thomas Paine. "*We have it in our power to begin the world all over again.*" I don't care how many mistakes we've made or how bad we think it is. By changing the course of our thoughts and actions in any moment, we change the wheel of causation. It is Law - the Law of Cause and Effect - and it is guaranteed. It is here in the new moment.

Affirmation:
I am free to begin again now.

6

We Do Know!

What is the first thing you do when you have an unexpected physical pain of some kind? It happened to me yesterday. I started to panic for a moment. Then I immediately went into Spiritual Mind Treatment.

I remember a day when I'd get a pain and I would panic and immediately think something was wrong. I don't do that anymore. I treat and wait for inner guidance on what to do next. It always comes. Everything I could ever want to know is inside of me and, if I approach everything from that standpoint, the answers always manifest.

Last night as I lay in bed with this pain and as I began to treat, it was as if I saw this shadow in my mind's eye covering the bed. It was like a mass of thoughts—not the most self-serving—that seemed to swallow up my Spirit. I continued to treat and finally found myself comfortably and peacefully asleep. I awoke with the pain slightly lingering and felt compelled to listen to Emma Curtis Hopkins' meditation, *The Radiant I Am*. Today, I am feeling much better and I stay open to more direction from within.

All the great mystics have encouraged us to go within for guidance and direction. They've said things like "*Know thyself!*" and "*The Kingdom of Heaven is within*," and "*All is mind*." It goes back as far as the beginning of civilization as we know it. There were always deep thinkers who inspired us to be confident in our inner knowing.

We still seem to deny the inner journey and I believe our

world demonstrates this. People strike out without thinking. We think we can solve our problems from the same energy that created them, when all the while there are spiritual solutions to everything. Emma Curtis Hopkins wrote, "*I know all I will ever know and it is time to make myself known.*" This doesn't mean that we are closed from future illumination. For me, it means that everything we could ever need to know is within and it is time to make that Self known, to reveal that information, to expand, to allow for further illumination.

Someone asked me yesterday how you can tell if something is your deep intuition or if it is not. There is a definite way you can tell. If your guidance is life-giving, creates more happiness for you and others, and feels good in a deep way, you can know that you are not being led astray.

We know when to call 911. We know when to pray. We know when to turn left or when to turn right. We know whatever it is we need to know.

Affirmation:
My intuition is real and I follow it.

7

You are the Face of God

In the philosophy that I practice, the Science of Mind and Spirit, I believe there is one Mind, one eternal Spirit in which we all live, move, and have in our being. Another name for it is "The Field" or "God." It is Infinite and it has always existed. This makes the most Spiritual sense to me.

Because there is only One, I am in unity with everything seen and unseen. I am in unity with everything that has ever been and ever will be. This same thing is true for every part of creation. The one Life, the one Mind, the one Spirit is expressing through me individually and uniquely. It is expressing through you the same way - individually and uniquely. There is only one me. There is only one you. However, we are made from the same Universal stuff and so is a plant, a tree, and the ocean. Everything swims together in the same Life Stuff.

Why is this important for me to know? Well, if this is true, which I believe it is, then everything I think and do is felt everywhere. As I make individual choices in my own life, it becomes a part of the whole consciousness.

In these challenging times in which we live, I believe it is important to make mental choices that are loving and benevolent even toward those who we say we are against. Our mental choices make a difference, and more of a difference when they are backed by emotion and feeling - negative or positive.

We cannot say we want love in our world and then hold our love back from this person or that person. We either love or we do not. Loving doesn't mean we sit back in a nonactive way and passively agree with everyone. It means that we see beyond our differences into the true essence of each person. That essence is always perfect Spirit, no matter what that person is expressing. The more we can truly focus on that true essence, the more it is felt everywhere and cannot help but be felt by that person.

When someone comes to me as a Spiritual Counselor and tells me they want another person to change, I can do nothing but change my own perspective. I see perfect Spirit everywhere and in everything. I am not responsible for how someone chooses to use their individuality, but I am responsible for how I engage with my mental attitude toward them. Life changes as we change our mental attitudes toward it. "*When you change the way you look at things, the things you look at change,*" wrote Wayne Dyer.

There is a song written by Karen Drucker called *You are the Face of God.* The words expressed are "*You are the face of God. I hold you in my heart. You are a part of me. You are the face of God.*" These are true words and if we can say them to each and every person (without condoning behavior), I believe we can begin to shift the consciousness of this planet.

Mother Teresa wrote, "*Seeking the Face of God in everything and everyone at all times, and the hand of God in every happening; this is what it means to be contemplative in the heart of the world.*"

Call it God, or call it what you will, it is one thing and we are all expressing it. This Presence never leaves us. The more we can see It everywhere, the more It will appear. I believe, as we sit in this loving state and listen deeply, we will be Divinely directed as to what is ours to do, to say, and to assist in the physical plane.

Affirmation:
I see the Face of God in everyone.

—16—

8

It Can Be a New Day

It is the last day of this month. I am putting this month to rest and giving birth to a new day. It has been both a wonderful month and a challenging month. So much has occurred. If I truly looked at each day with the eyes of awe, I would see that even in the challenges, it was a truly amazing month. However, this month is over and the new month is beginning.

I now get to start anew. I do not have to carry the old with me. Even if I remember it, I can choose to change my outlook on those memories. I can step back and look at them from a new perspective or I can let them go completely and just start over right now.

If I want to create something new—wonderful relationships, more abundance of finances, good health—it would be better if I started with a clean slate. I can choose to wipe my memory clean of the old thoughts that might dictate what can happen today.

I am dealing with an Unlimited Source that is undefined in this moment. I get to create the new mold for a new experience. I can know that any pain I feel, or sorrow about something I wish I'd done differently in the past, has no bearing on today. I am truly free.

When I was in theater school, we used to do an exercise where we would look at everything through the eyes of a newborn baby. We would pretend that we had no emotions or beliefs about anything. The teacher would instruct us to actually crawl around the floor and look at everything from that perspective of non-judgment. It was an amazing exercise and everything down to a ball of dust on the floor became a point of curiosity, wonder, and unlimited potential.

What if we could do that as we start this new month, this new day? What if we could begin to look at everything from a place of non-judgment and only with the desire to experience love? What if we were to look within ourselves and do the same thing? What if we were to let go of the shadows of yesterday, our mistakes that have no meaning today, and just start as newborn babies?

Jesus, the great Master metaphysician and teacher, once stated that unless we became as little children we can't enter the Kingdom of Heaven. Well, he also stated that the Kingdom of Heaven is within. I invite us to experience *our* Kingdom as little children would—with wonder, amazement, and unlimited possibilities. We can be anything we'd like to be in this moment, but we have to be willing to let go of the stories of old and begin anew. We hold the chalkboard, the chalk, and the eraser.

Affirmation:
I take a new look at everything today.

9

Love Epidemic

I am certain that we create our lives by contemplation. If we think about something long enough with feeling and emotion attached to it, it becomes our experience. We attract more and more of whatever that is into our lives.

I heard Bruce Lipton, the biologist and scientist, speak, and he stated that 95% of our lives are created from our subconscious and that only 5% of us is conscious. Most people do not even realize what and why they are doing something. Some old tape is playing from their childhood over and over. This might have been why Jesus spoke the words, *"Father forgive them, for they know not what they do."*

Many people want to go into their subconscious to try to find out what and why they are thinking something in order to change it. This is not really necessary. Bruce Lipton put it simply. He said, *"It's all very obvious. Just look at your life if you want to know what you are thinking."*

This is what we teach in our philosophy, the Science of Mind and Spirit. We know we are responsible for our life experience. Many are not attracted to this philosophy because of this. They do not want to believe this one simple thing. I am fully responsible for my life.

I know that I am responsible for my life. I am not responsible for your life, but I am responsible for my reactions to everything. I am responsible for my thoughts. I am responsible for how I use the precious gift of my mind. It is a powerful thing, and when I learn to use it on purpose with love, if "*I say to that mountain, move over there, it will move*" (Jesus, the Christ).

In today's times we are being called upon more than ever to use our minds on purpose with love. It is not easy when confronted with fear and hatred to turn to love. It's a beautiful day when so many stand together in love. "*What the world needs now is love, sweet love...not just for some, but for everyone*" (Hal David). That includes EVERYONE.

"What can I do?" is the cry of many. Every day, we are showing the world what we can do. Spirit creates by contemplation. Contemplation on _____ (you fill in the blank) will lead to action. It is called the Field of Cause and Effect. Let us go into our closets and contemplate, visualize, and fill our minds and hearts with Love and then walk into the world in action.

Let us begin right where we are with our families, friends, at the grocery store, at the Post Office, at the airport, and everywhere. It's happening. We are already creating an epidemic of love. Things might still confront us that make us look like we are losing, but that is the time to do our best work.

Ernest Holmes wrote, "*Give me one person who is for something and against nothing... and I will find another Jesus, another savior.*" We are all that one person - ALL OF US.

Affirmation:
I move into action from the highest consciousness of love.

10

Walking in the *I Am* Presence

When I become aware of the I Am Presence, It becomes aware of me. When I identify myself as It, It identifies Itself as me. I have heard this truth from many faiths and traditions. Many Master Teachers have spoken the words, "*I Am.*" What exactly does it mean?

As I meditate on these two words, something takes place within me. I begin to understand on a deeper level that *I Am nothing but Consciousness*. I am not my stories. I am not my thoughts. I am not even the thinker who thinks my thoughts. *I just Am.*

In the five steps of Spiritual Mind Treatment, I pray from the *I Am* consciousness, knowing that as I speak my words as Law, they become so. The most important step in this five-step prayer called Spiritual Mind Treatment, really the only step, is the first step—*God is All there is.* If I can truly speak these words, moving and living and breathing from this place, there are no other words to speak.

When the great teachers have stated there is a place where there is no desire, this is what they are speaking about. When we realize who and what we are, there is nothing to desire. We already have everything. All we are doing is expressing that everything by letting it flow through us into experience.

In the film, *Awake in the Dream*, Barbara Marx Hubbard spoke these words at the end (I am paraphrasing), *Visionaries, stay alive for a long time. The world needs you.*

What is a Visionary? A Visionary is someone who can see the world not as it is in form, but as it is perfect in the Spirit. Form is transient. The Spirit never changes. The Spirit is the Great I Am. The Visionary knows this. No matter what is occurring in the world of experience, the Visionary observes it as part of the unfolding of the Great I Am Presence. The Visionary doesn't fret or fear, but knows that if he/she can keep his/her I Am Presence poised, even the seeming chaos becomes the road of peace.

These words are from the famous poem by Max Ehrmann, *Desiderata*.

"Go placidly amidst the noise and haste and remember what peace there may be in silence. ...whether or not it is clear to you, the Universe is unfolding as it should."

This is a Universe of balance and order. Balance and order is unfolding in every moment. Chaos is the Universe finding balance and order. When we stay poised in the *I Am* Consciousness, we walk in unison, with balance, poised, and ready at all times to be of useful service to all when called upon. When we walk in the *I Am* Presence, we do not resist what is, we find balance in ourselves in what is.

Affirmation:
*I am a visionary and I walk
in the I Am Presence.*

11

Be A Bumble Bee

According to the law of aerodynamics, the bumblebee cannot fly, but a bumblebee does fly. I do not know all the specifics about why a bumblebee flies, but this I do know. Sometimes, we don't know everything about why something is so and it doesn't matter. What matters is that we stop saying, "I can't."

Just because so and so didn't do it, or we failed last time doesn't apply to now. We are as different as our thumbprint and if there is something we want to do in our lives, *"what we can conceive and believe, we can achieve"* (Napoleon Hill). I'm sure a bumblebee wasn't thinking much about the law of aerodynamics. It just needed to get where it was going.

We are held back many times because of the rules we place around ourselves. When people tell me that they didn't succeed or they tried or this stuff doesn't work, I know it is because they just let the naysayers outside and within themselves pull them down. They didn't have the audacity of a bumblebee to just fly.

It takes boldness and audacity to live the life of our dreams and many of us just don't think it's worth it. Is it too much trouble? Are we afraid of ridicule? I get it. However, I just want to say this. God is expressing through everything and everyone from the bumblebee to the galaxies. We all have a place in this. We shouldn't feel bad if we do not become the next Einstein or Mother Teresa. However, if we do not follow our dreams because of fear of anything, we might want to think again. Are we giving up a small part of ourselves, and then another and another, until we are living a life of "quiet desperation?"

It is never too late. Age, social status, and money are not worthy obstacles. There is no dream too big for God. The bigger our dream, the more God we glorify.

The first thing to remove from our way is the idea that there are any limitations. If the law of aerodynamics doesn't work for us, a new law will become known. It's always been there just waiting for someone to discover it. Why not you? Why not me? Life is about expansion. Life moves forward. We are Life. What bold step for Life can we take today?

Affirmation:
I take a bold step in the direction of my dreams.

12

What Did You...I Say?

We sing a chant at our Center for Spiritual Living, "*I am remembering who I am.*" Ernest Holmes wrote, "*...If today is the logical continuance of yesterday, then all the tomorrows that stretch down the vista of eternity will be a continuity of experiences and remembrances. There is no past, no present, no future, but merely a continuation of being.*"

Continuing to remember who we are is an eternal process, forever expanding. I am processing a retreat my husband and I facilitated last week. I am willing to take what I have experienced and integrate it into my being. This is what the continuation of life is to me. As I walk, "falling forward," I am continuing.

In my processing, something profound came to mind today that explains a lot to me about myself. When I was growing up I had a father who didn't let me speak. If I did, I was always told that I didn't know what I was talking about. Children will listen and I surely did. I can see that this statement continued with me for many years until I became conscious of it later in life.

Sometimes we do not know why we do the things we do. We feel somewhat robotic about them. However, we are not robots; everything has an origin and we either decide to take it in, or not. In this case, I took in my father's words as my truth. I can see now that I have struggled with the idea that what I have to say is worth something. Many times I have kept my mouth shut.

This week at the Hindu Monastery, I had completed a prayer out loud when the Swami suddenly looked at me and said, *"I've heard many prayers but never one equal to that one."* Now I suppose this comment could be taken in many ways, but I took it as a compliment. I continue to process his words. However, I have to be careful, as his words are not any more important to me than my father's words. I must remember that it doesn't matter what someone else thinks of me, whether it is empowering or dis-empowering, unless I make it important. What do I think?

Thomas Troward, a New Thought writer, wrote about the ruling hand of an iron destiny we can create if we do not change the wheel of causation. If we continue to turn the wheel of our lives based on what came before, we continue to create the same experiences. For me, if I continue to rely on the words of others for my self-worth, I will continue to need them just like Dumbo's feather.

In *The Radiant I AM*, Emma Curtis Hopkins wrote, *"I have been a listening disciple. I have let people and objects and activities come toward me and impinge upon me till I have been over-piled and mountain-covered with thoughts. But now I know that I AM at my own Center, authority over and through my universe."*

When will I grow my own wings? When will I believe what I believe? When will I know what I know? It will happen when I decree it so. I cannot know something until I know it. I cannot know it until it so resonates with me that I can use it to affect my life experience—until I can live it.

Other people's words can be wonderful or hurtful, but the only words that have power are the words I allow myself to speak to myself. All words are merely a continuation of my own evolution. Life is a mirror and reflects back to me what

I am thinking. This I cannot escape from. Swami or father came from the same source—ME—my mental equivalent.

13

My Inauguration Day

Emma Curtis Hopkins, a 19th century healer and teacher, wrote, *"... but who hath told himself that all the objects he beholds and all their movements also are but projections of his own judgment? He seems always to be a learner and a seeker until at the center of his consciousness the fact is suddenly proclaimed that he himself produced the world as it appears. Then he no longer listens to information from without; he authorizes from himself what he would see and hear and touch; even what he would know. ..."*

Emma writes this in her book, *The Radiant I AM*. She goes on to let us know that she has found from her own I AM Consciousness that she can emanate a world of Life, Love, Peace, and Harmony by speaking, writing, and living those enduring truths.

Yesterday, we visited with Sadasivanathaswami, one of the beautiful monks from the Hindu Monastery here on Kaua`i. He took us on a tour of the Monastery and spoke to us for over two hours. Much of what he shared with us was totally aligned with everything I believe and seek to live. One particular thing we discussed was we cannot control what happens to us; however, we can control our perception of what happens. When we do, we transmute the experience. If we look for the good in everything, it is good that will be our experience.

This is the way I have chosen to live my life. There is no good or evil. Life merely is what I declare it to be. I cannot step back far enough to see the whole picture of all experience, but when in brief glimpses I do, all stigma, dogma, and belief falls away and all that is left standing is Life. I have dominion over my perceptions, my thinking, and knowing. I do not have dominion over others and their experiences, their perceptions, etc. It's important to remember that.

I am beginning to understand that it might well be true that the old world is falling away. This isn't happening literally. It is happening in consciousness. When Jesus said, *"In my father's house there are many mansions,"* he was talking about planes of consciousness. We can be in the same room with someone else and be on different planes of consciousness.

"There is no good or evil but thinking makes it so," wrote Shakespeare. We are currently in this moment of swearing in a new president. We all have our feelings about this moment. Some are fearful, terrified. Some are joyful, elated. Some are just plain indifferent. I feel that I am about to embark on the greatest adventure.

Ernest Holmes, the founder of Religious Science once wrote, *"When things look the worst is the time to do our best work."* I say when things look the worst, I might want to look again. Perhaps what seems like the worst is just my time to step up and take responsibility for what I see. Perhaps it is time to change my perception and judgment and take responsibility for shifting my own consciousness by doing my spiritual work. Perhaps it is time, as Henry David Thoreau put it, *"... to live with the license of a higher order of beings."*

The definition of inauguration is "the act of putting a service, a person, a system, etc. into action." I, too, am being inaugurated today. I am putting my spiritual self into action. We can each have an inauguration day, every day.

Affirmation:
As I shift my perception, my experience changes for my good.

14

Believe It is Already So and It Shall Be So

"Life always becomes to us the particular thing we need when we believe that it becomes to us that particular thing" (Ernest Holmes).

On Saturday, January 21, I've decided to stand in solidarity with the women of our nation. We are marching for peace, for equality, for the safety of every human soul. Have you ever believed in something so strongly that you felt that you needed to march for it?

In my belief system, life is Infinite, but I can only use as much of the Infinite as I can understand and accept. In this case, I must believe that these rights that I am marching for already exist. I must become these rights in my mind and heart first. When I do this, I am activating the Law of my being that responds to me by bringing me new understanding. It brings me what I believe is already an accomplished fact. If I continue to tell myself I do not know or I do not understand or it is impossible, then *that* is what I get in return. It is the Universal Law of Attraction.

To experience these rights, I must become these rights. If I am to see this happen, I must believe it has already happened. I must stay open in every moment to new possibilities on every front. I must begin to think my life and live my life the way I want to live it. I must expand into greater possibilities every day. I must trust that I know all that I need to know in every moment.

I must drop all the possibilities of disasters. I don't want disasters in my life or in the world. I must stand up for something I do want and believe it is already so. In other words, I must believe it in order to see it.

I am not against anything or anyone, but I am for a world that works for everyone. I am not hoping for this world. I see this world as an already accomplished fact in the Mind that maketh all. I open myself up to allow it to happen through me. I become its Soul and then I put that Soul into action.

Affirmation:

I become that which I wish to see in the world.

15

Stepping Through the Door to the Self

My husband and I created and facilitate a workshop called *Flying Solo*. The participants all share a defining moment in their life through storytelling. I am honored to be part of the unveiling of truth as it flows through each person who dares to take this workshop.

Each person, in some unique way, steps into a moment in their lives that had been emotionally painful. As they step into it, I receive a strong message for myself. There is no way around pain. I must step into it. The way to transformation is that first step we take into those things that are uncomfortable to face. However, the fact that this particular thing has arisen in us is a sign that we are ready for it.

When the student is ready, the teacher appears. Teachers come in all forms with different faces. We cannot predict when they come or how they come. However, what I know for myself and others is that when they appear, we are ready or they wouldn't be here.

We are the ones we have been waiting for and what we are waiting for is here within us, ready to be transformed by us. Love is the purifier of all. It is hot Source Energy. It is the refiner's fire that creates the field of acceptance of a greater Self.

We do not have to be afraid to face our past or any feeling or emotion. We are loved, forgiven, and accepted before we even begin the journey. As we remember our true identity, we can clearly see that all has been for our highest good. We can see that we co-created the path we are on by partnering with our desire to know ourselves.

On the doorway to the temple it is written, "*Man, Know Thyself.*" The gateway into the inner temple is the revealing of that Self. It is the only way in and the door is always open.

Affirmation:
I know myself as perfect, whole and complete.

16

Love Will Always Have the Final Word

Martin Luther King, Jr. spoke these words, *"I refuse to accept the view that mankind is so tragically bound to the starless midnight of racism and war that the bright daybreak of peace and brotherhood can never be a reality. I believe that unarmed truth and unconditional love will have the final word."*

I do believe that unarmed truth and unconditional love will have the final word. Ernest Holmes wrote, *"Love is a Cosmic Force whose sweep is irresistible."* All these words are Truth to me. I cannot argue with Truth. My question is can I reveal the Truth within myself? That is healing.

We are the ones that we've been waiting for. We've heard it many times. We are the ones. I respect the great spiritual leaders and messiahs of our past. But how much longer can we rely on them? We are part of the great awakening and I am so excited. I believe I am here to be that unarmed truth and unconditional love. I believe we all are here to have the final word of love. However, we have to step out of the words into the action.

If *"Love is a Cosmic Force,"* and we are Love, then we are that Cosmic Force. This cannot mean just loving certain people who are easy to love, but we must be able to look a discordant fact in the face and reveal the truth that lies beyond it. We must see through everything to love. People's acts might be unloving, but it cannot destroy their True Essence. I believe it is my responsibility to see that Essence in every moment.

Let us continue to be inspired by Dr. King's words, "*Darkness cannot drive out darkness. Only Light can do that. Hate cannot drive out hate. Only love can do that.*" However, as I celebrate the courage and inspiration of Martin Luther King, Jr., I also celebrate my own courage and my own ability to inspire and love. I, too, have a dream. Today is the day to be willing to accept myself and all others as a Cosmic Force—Love.

Mahalo nui loa to all who step into the unarmed truth of unconditional love. We have already revealed the final word.

Affirmation:
Love is my final word today and always.

17

Gratitude: An Overused Word?

Upon awakening this morning, I heard Dr. Joe Dispenza and his famous quote, *"Gratitude is the ultimate state of receivership."* He was celebrating what he called his "Seven Days of Gratitude" as the beginning of the Holiday Season. My first reaction was what a wonderful idea; seven days to focus on gratitude as a state of being not linked to any particular cause. Gratitude just is.

I went into my meditation, following his instructions to put my hand on my heart and bring up the emotion of gratitude. It's easy for me to do this because I have so much for which to be grateful. But, what about when we feel we do not have anything to be grateful for? What if our life is seemingly a mess? What if we just had a great loss? What if we are sick? Can we still be grateful?

My answer is yes, because gratitude is not just a word and it does not signal that everything presently occurring in our life is okay, even when it feels like it is not. Gratitude is not a state of denial of what is happening in the world of form.

For me, instead, gratitude means that we accept life as a journey that is unfolding perfectly right now. Gratitude means we are in awe of all life's experiences and that we are simply blessing what is as a deepening to a greater now. Gratitude is the knowing that we are held safely in Life's keeping while led by that deeper part of ourselves to a greater experience. Gratitude is simply faith that right where we are is not permanent, but that we are always moving and changing and becoming more of our eternal selves. Gratitude is changing our perspective of this moment into a miracle, a miracle because we are in awe of the magnitude and eternal aspect of just being alive.

Gratitude can be an overused word. It superficially escapes our lips with no real meaning other than the Hallmark card meaning we've given it. However, as a practice of being in the present moment, no matter what is happening in our life, we can settle into the awe of living, opening the doors to peace and true fulfillment with ease and grace. As a form of nonresistance and of playing in the field of what is, with curiosity and surrender, with a trust and faith in the unknown, I believe it is an energetic bridge to oneness with everything and everyone. This gives new meaning to the famous quote by Meister Eckhart, *"If the only prayer you ever say in your entire life is thank you, that will be enough!"*

Affirmation:
Today I am grateful and that is enough.

18

Healing Isn't Fixing Things

As I sit here this morning, I am reflecting on what it means to heal. We've complicated a very simple process by telling ourselves that we have to fix something that is broken. If we could just look at this differently, everything would change.

We are not fixing anything. If we were, we would be like the surgeon who goes in and replaces parts of us and ties things together. This is what he/she does and I am happy and grateful for that.

However, Spiritual Mind Healing doesn't put things back together within us. Healing merely allows our innate Perfection to take over. Perhaps, we've forgotten it or we've covered it up with discordant thinking and stress.

As we remember who we are, we are undoing mental thoughts that bind us. When we do this, we naturally heal our bodies. Jesus was said to have cast out the devils from a person. What I believe he was doing was casting out the devils of thoughts that bound that person to think evil of himself. The person was set free by Jesus's loving consciousness.

Healing is revealing our Truth. I'm talking about Truth with a capital "T." You might not feel it right now, but that's where I come in as a Practitioner. Your Truth is that you are always wholeness. Your Spirit-Self has never been touched by anything. It is pure. Again, you might have forgotten this. When I remember it about you, something shifts in the Field (the Matrix, the one Mind) that we all live in. Wherever you are in consciousness, if you are willing to rise just a bit to allow the good stuff to penetrate those other not so good thoughts, you'll feel totally different.

Ernest Holmes once wrote, "*Water rises at the level of its own weight.*" Our thoughts do the same thing. They will rise as we let go of the weights that are holding them down. When we do, our bodies follow suit. It's science. I've witnessed many people heal through Spiritual Mind Healing.

So, the next time you are in a situation that you think you cannot change; it's true, you can't. The only thing you can change is the way you think about it. The more love and light you can allow to penetrate into the experience, the situation has to change because the person who is experiencing it (you) has changed.

Again, you are perfect. You are whole. You have a whole army of healthy cells of love that are more powerful than anything you could ever experience in the world of conditions. Allow them to sing and vibrate. I'll be cheering you on.

Affirmation:
I love myself unconditionally. I am whole.

19

Don't Give Up

Persistence and patience are two important qualities of successful living. So many times we give up right before success occurs. We might be trying a new business or just starting a new job or waiting for that new relationship. Patience and persistence are integral to manifesting our dreams.

But persistence is a tricky word. We might think being persistent means using willpower or forcing things to happen. This is far from the truth. Willpower does not bring our dreams of success any closer, but persistence in thinking the highest and best thoughts about our pursuits and ourselves does. This type of persistence is called "Will." When we say we have the will to do it, it means we are persistent in knowing that we are succeeding. We keep our mind poised on the dream and our vision of it coming into fruition. We do not get side-tracked by the world of effects that might show us otherwise. We look for what I call "signs of land." Signs of land are little clues the Universe drops in our view that show us we are going in the right direction. We won't see them if we do not look for them. What we focus on grows, remember!

My grandma used to say "Good things come to those who wait." I didn't like this at all. It made me feel even more impatient, especially if I was waiting for a boy to call me and he was taking his good time. I wanted things *now*. Our society teaches us the now mentality. For example, as fast as the Internet works, we can still wonder why it is not going fast enough. We are prepped for everything to be here now.

For me, patience is knowing, not waiting. It is knowing that all is well. It is knowing that even if something I am waiting for is not showing up in the now moment, I Know (with a capital K) that it is here already. Once I have claimed it, the Mind of the Universe (my mind) is cooking up the best way to bring it in my direction. I trust this. I have faith in this; therefore, I can be patient.

When we know what we want, when we remember who we are, and when we trust the Laws of the Universe, we naturally have all the patience and persistence to be successful. So, if we are having trouble with these two Ps, I invite us to go back to the beginning. Court the Universal Power, Source of All, God (or whatever you call it), focus inward and feel It breathe your breath and beat your heart. Love is there and you are that Love. It's just waiting for your willingness to recognize It. It wants to express through you in greater and greater ways.

Explore what is important to you and claim what you want. Don't relegate what you want to what you appear to have. Everything begins in the quantum field. Once you've decided, then give up everything that contradicts that want. Trust the Laws of the Universe. Remember that the higher Laws of the Universe always bring us the exact portion that we feel we can have. It's guaranteed.

Again, practice patience and persistence. Don't give up, ever! Changing direction is not giving up, and you will know if that is necessary. You are powerful! You are guaranteed to live the life of your dreams.

Affirmation:
I live the life of my dreams now.

20

Min(D)ing for Gold

"There is one life. That life is God's life. That life is perfect. That life is my life now"

Ernest Holmes

There is only One Life, everywhere present in everything, inexhaustible, and always recreating from itself anew. This is the Mind of God, the Eternal Source, the One Life within each of us. It is Love; it is Good.

Knowing this as Truth, I contemplate why there is so much suffering in the world. My answer is that many of us do not know and believe this about ourselves. So, my mission in life is to be one of those mentors who assists in bringing this message to those who are earnestly seeking it.

In life, when one mines for gold, he or she must explore, then drill, and then assess what has been drilled. They must extract and process their find until pure gold is revealed. I do not know all the ins and outs of real life gold mining, but I know that what lies within each of us is Gold. Taking out the "I", we reveal what that Gold is: It is God, Source, Life.

In his book, *Creative Mind and Success*, Ernest Holmes writes, *"Life is from within out and never from without inward. You are the Center of Power in your own life."* Just like in real life mining, min(D)ing for God is an inward process. To mind for God, we have to first accept that our Mind is God's Mind and that *"the same Mind that made a star,"* as Ernest Holmes wrote, *"is the Mind that we use."* As much of it as we are aware of is personified as us.

At one time, I lived a life of poverty because I did not understand this concept. There were min(D)ing steps for me. First, I had to understand the principle theoretically. Then, I had to take what I knew theoretically and begin applying it to my life. If I failed, I had to keep stripping away the self-sabotaging thoughts and acts I committed. Saying that I want something and inwardly feeling like I didn't deserve it would be an example of a self-sabotaging, subconscious act.

There is an exercise of looking at yourself in the mirror and saying to yourself, "I love and approve of you." It is taught by Louise Hay and other self-love mentors. Many of us don't like doing it, but this is min(D)ing for God. Self-love comes first, then knowing what we want, and then taking action from our highest place.

Ernest Holmes wrote, *"The Universe is filled with activity. There is motion everywhere. Nothing stands still. All activity comes from mind. If we want to be in line with things, we must move. This doesn't mean that we must strain or struggle, but we must be willing to do our part by letting the Law work though us."*

What is Law? It is simply the energetic Force that reacts to our feelings and emotions. It is Infinite Intelligence that awaits the impress of our thoughts. It is not outside of us; it is us. It knows how to put the pieces of our life together. It works when we stake our claim and move with our inner promptings.

Here are some steps I took from Ernest Holmes' book Creative Mind and Success. Please do not move to the next step until you have mastered the one before it.

1. Get quiet until you feel the Presence of Infinite

Intelligence within and around you. (Sometimes sitting in nature helps.)

2. Get a picture of what you desire. Know what you want.

3. Believe you are receiving it by giving thanks for it as if you already have it. Gratitude is key.

4. Then declare to yourself that you now know what to do even though you more than likely do not. There is a place within you that does know.

5. Do this every day until you get some direction. Before you go to sleep is a good time because your subconscious is open and receptive.

6. Never deny that it is working. Ideas will begin to take form. Synchronicities, seeming coincidences, and chance meetings will greet you. When they do, act upon them with conviction and faith.

When you apply and work on these principles, you will find yourself living a new life, even better than you imagined. Ernest Holmes wrote, "*Great things are done by people who think great thoughts and then go out into the world to make their dreams come true.*"

I invite those reading this to experiment with these Principles by trusting them and putting them into action. You are a Gold Mine, a God Mind!

Affirmation:

I am the Center of Power in my life.

21

Is My Day Always Unfolding Perfectly?

Yesterday morning, my husband and I did our daily Spiritual Mind Treatment before getting out of bed. In case you are unfamiliar with it, a Spiritual Mind Treatment is an affirmative prayer that moves energy in the direction of your particular desire. It impresses the Field or One Mind with that desire. It is magnetic in that it draws everything back to you in perfect alignment with your beliefs concerning that desire. Treatment changes beliefs when we identify what those beliefs are.

Well, I claimed our day to be one of peace, prosperity, ease, and flow. I claimed a deepening of our faith and, of course, guidance and direction. Were my beliefs in alignment with those claims? I would soon find out. In The Science of Mind, Ernest Holmes states, "*Treatment opens up the avenues of thought, expands the consciousness, and lets Reality through. It clarifies the mentality, removes the obstruction of thought and lets in the Light; it removes doubt and fear, in the realization of the Presence of Spirit, and is necessary while we are confronted by obstructions or obstacles.*"

Yesterday, I did find out how powerful Treatment really is. We completed our exercise program and all was on schedule for our day which included dinner with a friend. We ate breakfast and began the dishes, when suddenly out of nowhere, our kitchen sink became totally clogged. Try as we may, we couldn't get it unclogged. We did another Treatment for solution and then moved our feet by calling the landlord. The whole problem was solved by a plumber before the clock struck noon.

Three other things happened that would have made anyone feel that their morning Treatment for ease and flow was not effective. Without going into detail, there was a huge miscommunication at our Center, we got a notice from a billing company that we had not paid a bill that was already paid, and a package we'd been waiting for arrived opened, minus the contents.

Now, compared to what some people face on a daily basis, these things are small life happenings. However, small as they might seem, they were obstructing the day I envisioned. I could easily have thought my Treatment was null and void, but what I came to understand was that my day was indeed unfolding perfectly. "*When you change the way you look at things, the things you look at change*" (Wayne Dyer).

If "*treatment opens up the avenues of thought, expands the consciousness, and lets Reality through*," my day was right on target. Everything that occurred did just that and the clearing of the clogged drain was the perfect metaphor. There was something standing in the way of my perfect day but only in the world of form. In the mental world, I got total clarity of the things I still needed to release in order to manifest an even more perfect day. For example, the clogging of the drain brought up old triggers between our landlord and us. The undelivered package brought up the question of truly feeling deserving. The confusion at our Center gave us clarity on what we truly want for our ministry. The final unclogging of the drain let me know that I am still letting things go and *clarifying my mentality*.

I am at a place in my evolution where I find that everything

I encounter has a message from me, for me. I trust the Law that, as Ernest Holmes says, *"Life is a mirror reflecting back to the thinker what he thinks into it."* None of what happens in life is a punishment for being a bad girl or boy. Everything is for our expansion, growth, and deepening. We are always guarded, guided, and protected and yesterday proved that to me beyond a shadow of a doubt.

Playing on the field of life is like running with that ball to the finish line without dodging and getting knocked down. Instead, if we can accept the little bumps along the way as hints that something needs to shift in our thinking, we are then constantly growing and expanding by shifting direction.

Spiritual Mind Treatment most definitely works and my day yesterday proved it to me. My evening dinner with our friend was the perfect completion. It provided warmth, deliciousness, and the understanding that even after everything that had occurred, a shift took place and the night was perfect.

We have a Law of our being that is always working on our behalf; however, we have to work with it, not against it. Everything doesn't always play out like we think it should, but it always plays out perfectly if we allow it to, while openly and honestly seeking understanding.

Affirmation:
My life is unfolding perfectly now.

22

No Lies

Recently, I was at a dinner party where people began speaking about ancestry.com and DNA and such. I always love to share how I was brought up Italian, but came to find out my DNA is 63% Jewish. Talking about our heritage makes for great conversation, but it can sometimes go south, which it did that night. It went the way of the slavery in America, Black Lives Matter and a recent trial that sent the murderer of a Black man to jail. I choose to believe that things are getting better. If I don't, I'm adding to the backward times and not to the shift of consciousness and spiritual evolution I believe is taking place right now.

This all brings me to our stories and the stories we choose to tell over and over again. I love telling that story about my DNA, but does it really serve me? Am I going to do anything about it? Does it enhance my evolution? I suppose it could add a richness to my life to know this, but in Reality with a capital "R," I am not my DNA. I am a spiritual being with an eternal story that continues. I am Eternal Energy called Rita in this lifetime. My soul continues and moves forever forward.

I have witnessed many people, including myself at times, stuck in our stories and our DNA. We think we are trapped by the diseases of our family. We wait for ourselves to follow in our parents' footsteps. Really, we should be making new footprints from the endless possibilities in a Field of unlimited potential. We know enough now about where our stories have taken us to let them go forever. We can keep the memories, but those memories are not our identity in this now moment.

I am a Practitioner and when someone comes to me and begins to tell their story, I listen. I listen to the subtext of their story. Behind all our stories there is a belief that is trapping us in that story. I uncover it and I bring it out and forward so the person sees it for themselves. Once that happens, the lie is uncovered, and the truth is revealed. The person has the choice to let it go or keep on telling that story, holding it in place as a belief.

Every single story we tell is held by a belief. It might be a belief that we are unworthy. It might be a belief that we can never be enough. It might be a belief in poverty or that we are always enslaved to someone or something. However, the Truth will set us free.

The Truth is that everything is belief, and we make up these beliefs. They are either passed on to us or they come from our own experiences. If we could take a belief and truly see it as just that, a belief, we would be set free.

If all there is are beliefs and if beliefs create our lives, then why not choose ones that are going to create spectacular lives? You might think it is impossible. I know that it is not impossible because I've done it. I used to believe I was stupid. I used to believe that I wasn't enough. I had plenty of stories to prove it. I finally had enough of the life those beliefs were creating and I took those beliefs and turned them around. It wasn't easy; the spiritual life is not easy. However, it was worth every moment, every year that I spent working on it.

For me, there is only one belief that never needs to be changed and that is the belief that tells me my true DNA: Divine Nature Always. I am from a Divine Heritage that is perfect. It is all around me, through me, and in every cell in my body. I was created in perfection, no matter what my body looks like or who my parents were. I am Divine Perfection and so are you. When we begin to make this the basis of all our beliefs, we will tell ourselves no lies.

Affirmation:

My true Nature is always Divine.

23

I am Aware

Awareness is everything. Our awareness is what creates our life. What are you aware of? In a Deepak Chopra meditation I experienced, the mantra was, *"I am aware of being cared for and supported."* I taste these words by repeating them to myself until I feel them. I am comforted for sure.

I wonder how often we do not feel cared for and supported. Maybe we are in pain or having financial struggles or maybe our partner just left us. Can we say we feel cared for and supported? What about the state of the world right now? Do we feel cared for and supported?

The Truth I know tells me that awareness is everything and what I am aware of is showing up as my life. If I can trust the flow of life through me, especially when things aren't as I would like them to be, I am doing my best work. I can bring peace of mind to myself through knowing the Truth amidst my difficult times. I can change my experiences through my awareness.

One of the Principles of Huna, a metphysical theory proposed by Max Freedom Long, is that *energy flows where attention goes.* When I am in difficulty, more meditation and less focus on my difficulty changes the flow of my energy to my higher self. All the answers lie with my higher self, not with my conditional world. A refocus of attention changes everything.

I am taking more time this week to be quiet. I am taking more time to focus my awareness on the knowing that I am always cared for. I am taking more time this week to listen more deeply.

There is a deep call right now. I can hear it below the screams of tragedy and turmoil around us. It is asking me to go much deeper than I've been going. It is asking me to really take the time for this. It is asking me to talk less and listen more. It is asking me not to judge by appearances. It is asking me to love more.

One of the Principles that we state in the New Thought Philosophy is "*We believe the ultimate goal of life is to be a complete emancipation from all discord of every nature, and that this goal is sure to be attained by all.*"

The only place to begin the journey down this road is to begin it. We don't have to wait for others to achieve it. We can begin anytime. It begins with awareness. It begins with living in a peaceful state of mind first, not when everything is okay on the outside.

I think this mantra by Dr. Chopra is a good one. I think it is worth repeating and contemplating. "**I am aware of being cared for and supported.**"

Affirmation:
I am always aware of being cared for and supported.

24

Expanded Awareness

Deepak Chopra spoke these words today, "*You can't think, feel, or force yourself into expanded consciousness.*" How true this is and yet, so many times we get frustrated because we think we aren't getting it. It meaning a deeper spiritual awareness. We want everything to change quickly and we want what we want now. Deepak goes on to say it has taken thousands of years of study and meditation and spiritual practice for the mystics to come into expanded consciousness.

I get what he is saying, but I also know something else. It can happen right now. In fact, it already is or we wouldn't even be able to desire it. We are expanded consciousness. The question is, are we using it?

We can't "*think or force*" ourselves into expanded consciousness because it is a matter of letting go. Someone might ask, what are we letting go of? At one time, I would have said that we are letting go of the relative world or the world of form, but this is not true.

Now I believe we must accept the relative world as the result of our thoughts and perceptions. We must put the relative world in its proper place—the place of experiences. We are like artists who paint pictures. We are like writers who write stories and plays. We are masters of creation. We have peopled the relative world with all that is in alignment with our own vibration.

The other day when we held our labyrinth walk, I did an

experiment. There is a man who lives at the beach who can be loud and rather forceful. I had quite a time with him last month. In fact, he was the only one who came to our labyrinth walk. I accepted the idea that I was just there for that experience, that we had called each other together on some level. It must be, if what I am saying is true.

This time, I wanted a peaceful and quiet labyrinth walk for everyone who came. Before we started, my husband and I meditated and did a prayer treatment, knowing that only peace and love would enter our realm of experience. I breathed into and became the essence of peace and love, sending it out to the man who was nearby.

Well, the result was, he never came near us that day. In fact, he walked right by like he didn't even see our 24-foot labyrinth. My point is that we people our world from the inside out. We are the creators of our experience. I was going to have peace that day *with or without* my friend.

What is the expanded awareness that Deepak is speaking of? It is the knowing that we are part of something that far outlasts the world of form and experiences. It is eternal and unlimited. We are energy in form. We are vibration. We are unbounded. We are co-creators. We are Love. We live our lives of experience from the level of our vibrational energy. We can go no higher or further than we are. Fear begets more fear. Love begets love. If we want expanded experiences, we must expand our awareness into the Infinite. It is a matter of relaxing. It is a matter of letting go. It is a matter of surrender. It is a matter of Beingness.

Affirmation:
I expand my awareness into the Infinite Life.

25

Ancient Wisdom Is...

There is an Ancient Wisdom that is thousands and thousands of years old. In essence, it is:

1. Everything is consciousness and consciousness is in everything.

2. So above, so below and so below, so above.

3. The higher always incorporates the lower.

4. Awareness is a level or a degree of consciousness.

5. The highest awareness is the awareness of God in each person and each person in God.

6. We create our life by our choices.

When I read this in Tom Sannar's book *Quantum Wholeness*, something strongly came home to me. It was this: how easily we can forget the Truth because we believe what someone else tells us.

Think into your life. Is there something you believe that you feel someone could never take away from you? Think again. The Ancient Wisdom above was the Truth everyone knew and taught. It was the essence of their belief system. However, we have forgotten. How did we forget?

The good news is that it is in our cellular being and still in the Collective Consciousness. This is why it seems so familiar to us when we hear it told to us in different ways across cultures.

The Ancient Wisdom above is what we call New Thought today. And now we can see it is not new at all. We have forgotten the Ancient Wisdom because we have allowed others to tell us what the truth is and we have believed them. There were people who wanted power and so they sought to make us believe we were powerless, that things just happened to us. They told us that there was a God above that condemned us or rewarded us according to our deeds.

It's not their fault. We were the ones who believed everything they told us. However, now we are trying to get back to the Truth.

But think again! We do not need to get back to the Truth. The Truth just is. It has always been. No one took it away from us. We can begin with forgiveness of ourselves and of those who we feel victimized us. We can take responsibility for ourselves. We can love only! The Truth is here. It stands waiting for our awareness.

Now is the time. We get to choose what we believe. We get to remember who we are. We are in charge of the evolution of our own soul. The Light of inner awareness is ignited once again. The New Age is here. Everyone will arrive. There is no condemnation. God is right here in me and in you. We can never be separated.

Affirmation:
My inner awareness is ignited. God is me.

26

Checking in With My Faith

I love the definition of faith in the *Science of Mind* text. It *"is a mental attitude against which there is no longer any contradiction in the mind that entertains it."* In other words, I know that I know. I don't have to prove it to anyone. It is a deep abiding feeling of peace that all is well.

Of course, I can have faith in other things too. I can have faith that all will turn out terribly. Faith is. The opposite use of Faith is fear. We all have Faith. It is a matter of where we are placing it—how we are using it.

What a story we write for ourselves! We line up all the characters to play out the parts for us. When we can analyze everything down to a story with characters and realize that we are the writers, actor, and director, and that we can change the story, the healing begins.

In playwriting, every story has a major character that has an overall objective and character arc throughout the play. The major character learns something about himself and comes out the other end triumphant or not. Drama re-enacts life. When we can get to the cause of the story we want to change, and change the cause within ourselves to the truth about ourselves, a healing takes place.

For example, if I am not in right relationship with someone in my family, I do not go out and try to change them and get them to see my point of view. I must get in right relationship with myself. The love we feel for ourselves is the love we give to others. I must have faith that this self-love is revealed in all parts of my life now. I cannot attract something I am not.

Physical disease is prevalent because we have made it so. It fills the textbooks. It fills the advertising world. We are truly feeling this as we are in the midst of a pandemic right now in 2021. It is so real that it seems we cannot escape it. I believe we can stop trying to escape disease and instead have faith in health. Health, in Truth, is our natural way of being. The new Quantum Science tells us we are born to heal. Our bodies, organized and aligned by an Infinite Intelligence, are always perfect. If something is out of alignment in the world of conditions, we can have faith in the perfection of Spirit/ Infinite Intelligence to lead the way back to Wholeness.

Once I was in severe financial straits, nearly bankrupt. One day, something clicked inside me. I saw I was trying to punish myself for something else by not allowing myself to be free of debt. I got to the cause. I straightened my mind out about it and then proceeded to trust in the process of becoming debt-free. I had faith in my abundance and walked forth from that place.

The thing about life is to take 100% responsibility. We are the writer, the major character, and the director. At any moment, we can take up the pen, write a new story and have faith in a totally different ending. We can have faith because the Law of Cause and Effect, the Law of Mental Equivalents, the Law of Correspondence brings back to us exactly what we put into it. It can be done with ease, with grace, and with love. I have faith in this way of being.

Affirmation:

I author my success story and live it.

27

She Was Tired of
Giving In

It was the end of a long day at work. Rosa Parks was tired. She got on the bus to go home when the driver told her to make room for white passengers and move to the back of the bus. Rosa Parks' simple refusal that day spurred on the Civil Rights Movement in the United States. Later, Rosa recalled that her refusal wasn't because she was physically tired, but that she was tired of giving in.

Do you ever get tired of giving in to old beliefs that are not serving your life? Rosa Parks was tired of giving in to what always had been and she began a whole new chain of causation. In other words, her courageous act changed the direction of a whole belief system.

Collective consciousness or race consciousness are the beliefs held by the majority of the people in a country, a town, or even the world. These beliefs aren't necessarily truth; we've just accepted them for so long, they appear to be truth. We have the opportunity in every moment to let go of things we've given into and held on to. It's not easy to think differently or to let go of the old. Are you willing, like Rosa Parks, to go first?

"It is done unto us as we believe," said the mystic, Jesus. I know I have the opportunity to change my beliefs about the things that have always been. For example, the women in my family didn't drive. I could have followed suit. I almost did. However, one day I said, *"Of course, I can drive. How am I going*

to get around if I don't?"

There are many beliefs held by the majority of humanity. There are beliefs that disease is inevitable. There are beliefs that being rich is reserved for the minority. There are beliefs that there is not enough food in the world. There are beliefs that the ocean is poisoned and we are doomed. Of course, there are beliefs that benefit us also, but I'm talking about the ones that are keeping us in a negative spiral like hamsters on a wheel.

Rosa Parks ignited the change because she was *"just tired of giving in."* To tell you the truth, I'm tired of giving in too. I am tired of giving in to the ideas that keep me in bondage. I am tired of giving in to the ideas that tell me it is impossible to do this or that. I am tired of giving in to anything that is keeping my life down.

I'm willing to let go and take the leap into a new way of thinking. I'm willing to live a new idea about everything in my life that holds me back from expressing my Divinity at its highest possibility. It takes stepping away from appearances. It takes realizing that just because it's always been doesn't mean it always has to be. It takes a whole new idea.

I invite us to consider looking at what we are giving in to that doesn't serve the highest good for our life. After identifying what it is, I invite us to consider changing the belief behind whatever it is to its opposite. It's all made up. We made it up and we can unmake it now and create something greater. Rosa went first. Are you willing?

Affirmation:
I only give in to my highest Good.

28

Do I Accept It?

It is the mold of our acceptance that creates our reality. The question is *what can we accept as ours*? Everything is already here. Nature gives all: Love, Grace, Beauty, Power, Light, Wisdom, Joy, Peace - it is all ours. There is nothing to which we do not have access because we are the Universe and the Universe is in us. As the mystic, Rumi, wrote, "*You are not a drop in the ocean.* **You are the entire ocean in a drop.**"

We are not reaching for anything; we are merely revealing it all. The most important thing we can do is to work on ourselves first. What do we feel that we deserve? This is not about acquiring things or money or friends or power. It is about revealing the prosperity, the love, the friend that we are. It is about mentally removing the veil that covers up our authentic self and accepting our true self. It is about living from a place that accepts ourselves as the Good we seek.

We have to be definite too. I can find myself nonspecific about the things I want to experience. I just think, "*Oh, I want some of that,*" or "*I want to feel like that.*" It is not direct. It has no conviction about it. Specificity is important. When we are not specific, we live a cloudy life. We get a little of this or that, but we drift. We depend on the dreams of others while our dreams remain in a dream state.

For me, the formula, if there was one, is to know myself first and practice feeling the Presence deep within my being. Then, I must open up to Divine intuition. I must allow it to flow through me and follow that inspiration. Next, I must get specific about the particular experience I want. I must accept it as mine. I must open up my whole heart to it. I don't need to know how it will come about; I only need to accept that it has already happened.

I have witnessed this in my own life and in the lives of others. When we let go without fear, when we stop waiting for something outside of ourselves to make it happen, when we are clear, when we accept the Good, life unfolds accordingly. The Universe moves mountains through us. Remember, Life can only do *for us*, what It can do *through* us.

Try this as a daily prayer: *I have great gratitude for my life. I accept Good as a natural part of my expression, as an individualization of the One Spirit through and as me. I accept Life unfolding through me at its highest expression. The mold of my acceptance is growing every day. And so It is!*

Affirmation:
I accept Life unfolding through me at its highest expression.

29

Why Do I Want to Live?

Why do I want to live? This is the question that came up yesterday in a conversation between my husband and me. We have both experienced this deep question with clients and friends who have been ill.

I think it is a very good question to ask ourselves often. "*Why do I want to live?*" Of course, I understand at a deep level that I am immortal and I will always live. Life is. We cannot fight for our lives, nor can we get life. It simply is. However, we are here and we are living on the earth plane. Why do we want to continue here?

Many will give reasons like, "*I want to see my grandchildren grow up,*" or "*My children need me...my partner needs me,*" or "*I still have something to do.*" Some people will give you their bucket lists. Some people are just afraid of death. Some people are afraid for the people they will leave behind. I, too, want to live because I believe I am of assistance in a myriad of ways here. But I feel that a deeper probing might be very worthwhile.

I believe that earth is the best place to learn and experience my awakening to God because I have to really go within and trust the unseen. I have to truly have faith and test the Principles against all odds. I am learning to be satisfied with just "being."

Anita Moorjani, who wrote *Dying to Be Me*, spoke of her experience of "Oneness" in the field between life and death. She then came back to tell us we could experience that exquisite feeling here on earth and live from that place. I want to live because of that. I want to experience the Spirit, Mind, and Body all at once at the highest level possible.

I will continue to ask myself this question. If I am truly honest, there is a lot to be discovered in the answer. Why do I want to live? Perhaps, it is to truly embody Life without any reason at all, except to live.

Ernest Holmes once wrote: *"Man does not exist to leave a lasting impression upon his environment. Not at all. It is not necessary that we leave any impression. It is not necessary, if we should pass on tonight, that anyone should remember that we have ever lived. All that means anything is that while we live, WE LIVE, and wherever we go from here we shall keep on living. …We don't have to move the world...It will move anyway..."*

Affirmation:
I live to experience Spirit, Mind, and Body at the highest level possible now.

30

My Feelings Matter

What if you knew that everything you felt deeply could be felt by everyone? I mean everything you really felt, not just a passing thought or word.

This week, I got word that someone I knew was in a precarious situation. The details are not necessary. I do not know this person well, but I do care for their well-being. I couldn't contact them; all I could do was pray.

Now, prayer to me is not beseeching. It's called Spiritual Mind Treatment. It is speaking the solution or knowing that all is well because God, or Good, is in and through all, and nothing can be separated from the one Source. It is about giving gratitude for the successful outcome and then letting the result go for the Universe to unfold it perfectly. Prayer is knowing this about another person in my own mind. When I do this, because we live in one Field of Energy, it is felt everywhere. This is not woo-woo; it is physics.

Yesterday, when I prayed for this person, what came to my mind was Love. I knew in my own heart she was pure Love. She was Love, and therefore Loved. I felt Love rising up in me and I knew it about her. As Ernest Holmes once wrote, "*Love is a Cosmic force whose sweep is irresistible.*" I knew this person as that Force. I felt it deeply.

Almost immediately after my prayer, I heard this person was okay. All the details were not available, but she was okay. Could my prayer have been felt? I believe it was. This is what synchronicity is all about and we all experience it.

This is a feeling Universe. It is our deep, passionate feelings about anything that bring about that particular thing. Our feelings can be positive or they can be negative. No matter what they are, when they are strongly felt, they add to the energy field.

Do we want to add negativity or positivity? Please do not mistake what I am saying for bypassing our feelings. We should feel what we are feeling. We should go deep into our feelings because behind them are our beliefs. If we want to change our beliefs, our feelings will take us there.

If I had been scared for that person I just spoke about and continued to wallow in that fear, I would have been adding to the fear in the situation. This is true now as we focus on the world and its challenges. The fact that even one of us can rise above fear changes the consciousness of the whole.

For me, it is important to start right where I am and begin to change myself. As I change myself and the way I think and feel about things, I know I change the world. Gandhi knew it. Jesus knew it. All great mystics knew it. It starts with each of us, in our own minds, in our own hearts. As Ernest Holmes wrote, "*One alone in consciousness with the Infinite constitutes a complete majority.*" You matter, and your feelings matter.

Affirmation:
I live my life knowing I matter.

31

The Miracle of Parking Spots

Yesterday, my daughter and granddaughters and I went to the zoo. We drove around and around looking for a parking space. My daughter knew Religious Scientists are known for manifesting parking spots. It's a little joke, but it's true. She turned to me and said, *"Why don't you do what your people do, you know, get us a parking spot?"* I started laughing and I thought this must be what Jesus felt when he was at the wedding and his mom said, *"Why don't you make us a little wine; there's none left."*

My daughter and I joked about it and then I stated seriously, *"Here is what I know... we have a plan to take these girls to the zoo and there is no way we are going to be able to do that without a place to park. We require it and so I know we have a parking spot."*

Just then a parking space opened up. Wide-eyed, my daughter said, *"Mom, in the shade, too. Pretty good."*

Demonstrating a parking spot, although a small thing compared to the graver things in life, still makes a point. When we call upon the Universe and unite with It, there is an immediate answer. It is not a miracle. It is normal. Miracles are commonplace to us when we know the Truth.

Ernest Holmes writes: *"There is a point in the supreme moment of realization where the individual merges with the Universe...where the Oneness of all Life so enters his being that there is no sense of otherness. It is here that the mentality performs seeming miracles, because there is nothing to hinder the Whole from coming through."*

Enjoy this affirmative prayer for today. *Miracles are my birthright for I am one with the only Power. The same Power that made the stars and keeps the planets spinning, that made the tiniest insect and its intricate wings and the immense beauty of the Grand Canyon, is my Power now and always. I am Life itself. There is no separation. I am forever in sync with everything I could ever require. I already have it. I am heir to a Kingdom. There is never a need that is not fulfilled when I know who I am. I stay steadfast in this knowing. I rejoice in it. I breathe it in and I am fully emerged in God energy. I am Love, Peace, Abundance, Creativity, Perfection. Everything is here within me and surrounding me always and forever. I act from this place today and I am transformed.*

And with a grateful heart for parking spots and more, and for the knowing of who I am, I simply release my word as Law, knowing it is done, as I say, "And so IT is!"

Affirmation:
Everything is here within me and surrounding me always and forever.

32

Outside the Linear

While meditating this morning, I was reminded about not thinking linearly. What a mistake this is. I've done it too. When thinking through a problem to a solution, I think linearly. I am stuck in trying to change in the world of conditions. For example, I think something like this: first, this must happen, then I must do this, and then wait for this to happen, and then do this, then wait for them to do that before I do this, etc., etc., etc.

Life never quite works this way for me and it really slows me down. I do know better. It is only when I focus my attention clearly on my desire, moving with the flow, and stepping out of the way of the how it will come about, that miracles occur. When I realize that whatever it is that I am desiring is already accomplished, miracles occur. It is only when I act from the place of knowing that I am infinite and moving as Infinite Power that miracles occur.

When I say miracles, I mean those moments of synchronicity when everything comes together; when people, places and things rise up to meet my intention with ease and grace.

We live in a Field of Energy that is constantly molded and remolded in accordance to our thoughts, feelings, and beliefs. It is when I can stay clear and open to the unlimited possibilities in every moment and let go of the linear that the earth moves for and through me.

The other important ingredient to this is the ability to let go of the small stuff that blocks our flow. Forgiveness, Love and the ever-expanding awareness of my True nature and the True nature of each and every part of creation allows me to let go and live unrestricted by the past and future.

The linear is something we invented in this time-space-continuum. Our True nature is immortal, timeless, unlimited, and unbounded. Can I stay in this unborn moment, trusting my Infinite nature and truly believing in what I cannot see? If so, I will have stepped out of the linear and into the place of unlimited possibilities now.

Affirmation:
I step out of the linear and into the field of unlimited possibilities now.

33

Prayer Works

One thing I know beyond a shadow of a doubt is that Prayer works. I witness the power of Prayer in a multitude of experiences every day. **PRAYER WORKS**.

Ernest Holmes writes that our prayers do nothing to change God. God can't change. Prayer changes us. God is God. It is always here, right where I am and right where you are. God is Life and cannot be depleted or halted. Life is. Prayer changes our mind and, therefore, we are able to experience God at a higher level through a change in consciousness.

A few years back when I was sick, I didn't try to resist my illness. Instead, I kept remembering my Divinity. In the present moment, I am wholeness because this is what God is. I had the help of others. Sometimes, we need another person's faith to join us, perhaps when we are not totally strong. There is nothing wrong with that nor does it show weakness of any kind. Finally, one day, I rose from the bed and I knew I was healed.

I am talking about physical health now, but there are other dis-eases that prayer can heal. We might be in a financial crisis. We might want to pray for our country. We might want better relationships or a new home. It really doesn't matter because there is no big or small. Nothing is *more* spiritual. Everything is spiritual and we should experience the most wonderful and healthy abundant life.

However, we cannot have a healthy, abundant life without a mental equivalent. We can't have monetary prosperity if we lament about being poor all the time. Prayer works but we have to come from a place of faith that the outcome is already complete. We have to taste it and feel it. If we can't move ourselves that far, we have to just trust and take a mental leap of faith into the unseen.

There is an Energy Force (I call it Law) that moves within us, bringing everything forward into manifestation. Our thoughts are powerful, but as Dr. Holmes wrote, "*Trained thought is more powerful than untrained thought.*" Prayer assists us to train our thoughts in the direction of the life we want to live. If we keep at it with gratitude for what is here now, and if we have faith and trust and do not falter, what seem like miracles occur. They are not really miracles; they are the normal occurrences of a mind and heart that accepts their Good.

This week, I invite us to pray often for our Good, for the Good of our friends and family, for the Good of our country and of the world. Trust that everything is unfolding perfectly. Look for the miracles. They are here.

Affirmation:
My prayers are powerful and fully realized.

34

My Thoughts on January 6, 2021

I've been here in time and space for 67 years. From the assassination of President John F. Kennedy to September 11, 2001, I've experienced violence upon violence in our country and around the world. However, yesterday was the first time that I was deeply frightened. The sight of an angry mob climbing our Capitol walls and freely walking within its corridors against the background of the paintings and statues of American history, with only one intention - the violent upheaval of American democracy- was more than disturbing. To think that this upheaval was instigated by the encouragement of the highest leader in our government made me shiver and cry. What was mine to do?

I wanted to call Washington. I wanted to rush there and protect our government officials who were just doing their jobs. I wanted to kick and scream, "*Stop! Stop! Stop!*" However, in that moment, I remembered what Mother Teresa once said, "*Grow where you are planted.*" I am planted on an island here in the middle of the Pacific Ocean. My stewardship is a Spiritual Center and its global community. My job was to pray and be here for those who were frightened and sad. My job was to get past my fears and stand tall. My job was to hold what we call "The High Watch" for the rest of the world. (The High Watch is about holding the Consciousness of Peace and Love amidst the turmoil of the outer world.)

People say that praying isn't enough. There is truth in that statement if we do not put action behind those prayers. In yesterday's (January 6) moment, that is where I began. Those prayers led us to hold a peace vigil last night. I know that different Faiths and Faith leaders around the world were doing the same thing. It makes a difference, for Consciousness is aback of everything.

Yesterday's violence in Washington was an effect of consciousness. It couldn't have happened if it wasn't backed by the consciousness of the majority of us. We have to admit that we've been in turmoil over this election for a long time. The wheels of causation were set into motion for something to explode.

However, as I know, the wheels of causation can be turned in the opposite direction anytime we decide to do so. And, yesterday we did. The consciousness of peace and justice and love was greater than the consciousness to obstruct that justice through violence. In turn, the people - our police force, our national guard, our secret service, our fire department (all effects of consciousness) came in to quell the fires of violence and bring peace to the experience. I am so grateful.

There is more to this epic story and all is not resolved in the world of effects. But after yesterday, I know we are up for whatever comes. I know that the consciousness of Love is stronger than its opposite and it will pierce through, truth will rise, and peace is here now. The will to uphold democracy rose yesterday and stood behind our government officials and all who assisted. The last year of challenges (COVID-19 and more) has brought us to a "this is enough" attitude. The majority of our population, I believe, is ready to communicate in peace and work in Unity.

Mr. Rogers is quoted as saying, "*In scary times, look for the helpers."* We all did our part. We were all helpers yesterday. We prayed. We consoled the frightened. We took to the streets and put ourselves in harm's way to make sure peace and justice were served. We should be proud of ourselves and all involved. We are strong. We are Love.

And for those who feel wronged about yesterday, who still want something different than what it is, remember what Ernest Holmes wrote. *"Love is a Cosmic Force whose sweep is irresistible."* Ask yourself if your cause is backed by love, true love, unconditional love, the kind of Love that respects and includes everyone and everything, the kind of Love the endures no matter what the outside storm.

Dr. Martin Luther King, Jr. put it best, *"I have decided to stick with love. Hate is too great a burden to bear. ...Love is the only force capable of transforming an enemy into a friend. ...Darkness cannot drive out darkness; only light can do that. Hate cannot drive out hate; only love can do that."*

Walk! March! Do what you need to do. Make your truth known, but let it be backed by love.

Affirmation:
My life is expressed only as unconditional love.

35

The Abundance Prayer

This morning I experienced an abundance meditation and read Ernest Holmes' Abundance Prayer on page 264 of the *Science of Mind* text. At this time in our world when so many are focused on their ability to provide, when many have lost jobs, or paychecks have been cut back, it might be a good time to focus on Abundance.

The beautiful thing about Abundance is that it has nothing to do with what is in your bank account. Abundance is the belief in the Energy and Substance of Source/God that is always moving through us. Once we open up to recognize It as our Source, it releases the stranglehold we have on focusing outward and waiting for our abundance to show up. We realize that Abundance is an inside job.

If it seems abstract or if it seems like it is just a nice idea, I invite you to try it for forty days, ideally. If you earnestly apply yourself, the results are immediate. There is a book called *The Abundance Project* by John Randolph Price that is foolproof. A daily meditation for even ten minutes focused on your inward Infinite Supply brings forth changes immediately.

Why is all this so? Well, it is scientific. As you change your beliefs, your thoughts change because your brain changes. You are literally rewiring old thought habits with new ones. Your energy changes and what you attract to yourself changes.

Here is a simple Abundance Prayer. Sit quietly, slow your

breath down and focus in your heart space.

There is only one Spirit, one Energy, one Source. It is Spiritual Substance always taking form as supply as my life. All that I experience is flowing from this Infinite Substance that flows within me and must take form. I trust this ever-present activity within me and know that everything in my life is led by Divine Right Action. I know what to do in every moment. I am guided and directed by Source into Right Action at all times. I attract continuous support and love and supply. Abundance is mine because I am Abundance. I experience a life of Abundance right here and now. I am ever grateful for what is already present, knowing that right in this moment it is already expanding as my forever supply. My Word is Law and is fulfilled. I open up and allow all to flow to me and through me for the highest Good of all. I release this Word of Abundance into the Universal Flow as Law. And so it is.

Affirmation:
Abundance is mine because I am Abundance.

36

You are Invited to a Potluck

On the Island of Kaua`i, potlucks are the most popular way of getting together. It works because it takes the burden off the host of having to provide everything for a large gathering. We love to get together in large gatherings.

During the COVID-19 Pandemic, there was a halt on potlucks at our Center. Our Thanksgiving Potluck was canceled. Our women's group potluck didn't take place and our Christmas Sunday potluck was put on the back burner until another year. So, what are we left with? The memories of potlucks of years gone by. I'm sure they will come back again, but for now I want to focus on a different kind of potluck. It is the potluck that takes place in our mind in every moment.

In the New Thought teaching, we know there is, as Ralph Waldo Emerson put it, *"One Mind Common to all people."* We all share one Mind of Infinite Intelligence. We might call it the Collective Consciousness or Race Mind. It is the Mind of God in Action, meaning that it is aback of all creation. We are contributing to it and using it every day. It is a sort of potluck of all thought that has ever been thought and all experiences that have ever been felt for eons. We are born into it and it may or may not run our lives.

Have you ever walked into a room of people and felt the atmosphere? Have you felt drained after being with certain people, or uplifted for that matter? We are all thought and we are transferring thought to one another all the time. This is why it is important to become a conscious and responsible potluck contributor. What are you bringing to the table and what are you taking from it?

At a food potluck, we make these choices very deliberately. We bring our favorite things or those that are easiest to prepare or buy. Some of us are nutritionists, some are vegans, vegetarians, or carnivores. We like sweets or we stay away from them. We are all individuals and we make conscious choices about our food contributions and also of what we will eat.

I invite us to do the same at our potluck of the mind. Let us be conscious of what we bring to the table and also what we choose to accept or reject. There are a lot of different ideas, beliefs, and thoughts to choose from. We have the Power to accept or reject because we are at choice at all times. Why would we be able to choose what kind of food we eat and not be able to choose what kind of thoughts we think? We are beings of volition and choice and that means in all areas of our life.

During this season of limited food potlucks, enjoy a luscious, positive, and loving potluck of the mind with each other. Bring the joy, receive the joy, and drop the negativity in the trash where it belongs.

Affirmation:
I choose uplifting thoughts for myself and for the world.

37

Offensive or Defensive?

Do you live an offensive or defensive life? Do you spend your time defending what you are doing? Do you second-guess your decisions? Do you defend your decisions to yourself and others or do you move through life with determination and conviction?

I don't know a lot about football, but I do know there is the offense and the defense. I know there is a lot more to it, but I'll simplify it for the sake of this blog. The offense keeps its attention on getting the ball to the goal and the defense makes sure the opposite team stays out of the way.

I can see how this relates to life and our goals and dreams. If we live in either of these extreme states of mind, we are either spending our time focused on positive thinking, visioning, and working toward those visions or we are defending to ourselves and others why we want what we want and possibly sabotaging our efforts every step of the way.

I can also see that having both states of mind can be helpful. If we are offensive creators, we are focused and directed. The only defense we might practice is denying and negating any beliefs or thoughts that stand in the way of those goals. Just like the defense in football, it takes a lot of strength and attention to do this.

I believe we have a team within us that works together at all times for our highest good. It is run by our Consciousness. It is both offensive and defensive. For example, keeping a healthy immune system takes offensive and defensive thinking and practice. Being positive is more than just thinking positive thoughts; it is negating any beliefs that stand in the way of love. It is taking action based on those beliefs.

Truly, we have everything we require to live a powerful, health-filled, resilient, and love-centered life. No matter what is happening in the outside world, our inner love army is always making sure we have every answer we require, have the inner strength to endure dark times, and an immune system that is strong, provided we nurture and nourish it. That nourishment includes both spiritual practice and good nutrition.

As we live through these more than interesting times, I invite us to call up our whole team—the offensive and the defensive—and let the only goal line be love. As the many systems and strategies fall away, as the world is coming to realize that what never worked is never going to work, we must give birth to those new strategies to create a world that works for everyone for the highest good.

It takes lots of practice and it isn't easy to produce a winning team in football. Likewise, living the spiritual life is not for the weak of heart. If we are here on earth, I believe there is something very special that is ours to be and do. Our own spiritual evolution is the world's evolution. We do not have to defend whatever that is. We just need to focus our attention on it and put it into action to bring peace to the earth plane.

Affirmation:
I play the game of life with love as my goal.

38

In the Womb

No matter the outcome of the upcoming election, whether I am blue or red or no color at all, there is something I must know now. What is that something? I must know that no matter what transpires, all is well. If the Universe is always conspiring in our favor, and I believe it is, then whatever the outcome is would have to be for our highest good, even beyond what we see on the surface.

Joseph de Maistra, a French lawyer, diplomat, writer and philosopher of the 18th century was quoted as saying, "*Every nation gets the government they deserve.*" I am taking this statement and translating it to what we call in Science of Mind—the Mental Equivalent. In order to manifest the life that we desire, we must have a mental equivalent of it. We must create a spiritual prototype for it. We must believe we can have it. We must act as though we do have it. We must walk through life as if it is already true.

I just listened to an impassioned speech by the Sikh American civil rights lawyer, Valerie Kaur, who is known for her speech, "Breathe and Push." She speaks about the rise of racism and hate crimes after September 11, 2001, that peaked for her when a Sikh friend was murdered. As a mother, she asks herself about the rise in racism today, "*What if this darkness is not the darkness of the tomb, but the darkness of the womb? What if our America is not dead but a country that is waiting to be born.*"

If we are a country waiting to be born and if we are a country that has the government it deserves, then it seems that the next best thing for all of us to do is to nurture the values that will bring about a birth filled with compassion, love, respect for diversity, mercy, justice, freedom, and even more. This should be our mental equivalent. Can we envision it? Can we live it now, even before we see it?

One of the most disturbing things for me that is occurring right now is our ability to turn against each other in the wake of the elections and COVID-19. When I hear us talking about how we are afraid of each other and the possibility of illness just because we come from somewhere else, or because our skin is a different color, or we have a difference of opinion, I can see how we are a microcosm of the macrocosm. If we want a loving, intelligent government, then we must provide the love and the intelligence to everything we are. We must think things through from the highest place before we act.

With the election less than two weeks away, what are we doing to provide a more loving country? Are we in good relationship with our families? With our neighbors? With ourselves? Are we willing to allow people to have a different opinion and still have peaceful conversation with each other?

I voted last week and posted on Facebook to encourage others to do the same. The only question posed to me was "*Did you vote for the good guy or the bad guy?*" One person's good is another person's bad? Can we handle that? How do we listen without judgment and still voice what we believe? How do we stay in love? Can we seek to understand without judgment?

I invite us all to perhaps look at this time with different eyes. There could be more than meets the eye. As Ms. Kaur stated, "Is it a tomb or a womb?" Childbirth is usually painful, and at the very end, as Ms. Kaur said, we are commanded to breathe and then to push. Having experienced it myself, I know we are called upon to surrender to the new life that is coming. As we breathe in all that is occurring in our world, can we push through it into a higher expression of ourselves? Can we surrender to our highest and best selves? The way we choose to look at the world and the way we choose to act in every moment will create our mental equivalent and everything that follows.

I invite us this week before the election to open our hearts, speak our word with compassion, listen with an open mind, and breathe and push all the love we have into the world, into the new, into life.

Affirmation:
I breathe and push only love into life, into the world, into the new.

39

Healing is Here

"We believe that we are surrounded by the Creative Mind which receives the direct impress of our thought and acts upon it. We believe in the healing of the sick through the power of this Mind. We believe in the control of conditions through the power of this Mind" (Ernest Holmes)

This Mind we speak of is the Mind of God in Action that works through each and every one of us; the Law of our Being that can bring healing to our lives. That healing comes with the realization that we are one with this Mind and that we are innately perfect. Our essence is perfect although we sometimes wear a cloak of imperfection.

I believe in this Truth and have proved it in my life many times. I am a spiritual scientist and am always seeking to prove the Principle of Perfect Health. *"There is no great and no small To the Soul that maketh all; And where it cometh, all things are; And it cometh everywhere"* (Ralph Waldo Emerson).

I was born into a genetic lineage of breast cancer. Every time I go to the doctor, they ask me about my history. It's in my records. The doctor always lets me know that my mother was a breast cancer survivor, as was my grandmother. This is true in the world of facts and I understand that because of this genetic code within my family, I have a tendency to repeat this illness in my own life.

However, the new science (epigenetics) tells me that I only have a tendency to repeat my history. There is also the capacity within me to go beyond my genetics, with the correct emotional, spiritual, and physical support, and change them. I turn my genes on and off as I interact with the environment.

Before I knew this, I cannot tell you how many times over the years I was threatened by the imminent danger of approaching breast cancer. I can't tell you how many times a doctor would say he felt a nodule and sent me off for a mammogram, only to find nothing. I can't tell you how many times I was told I had cystic breasts and I had to stay on top of it. I chose to look at these doctors as expressing care for me and this led me to have a mammogram every year since I was forty.

Then, one day something within me changed. I had been sent off to Oahu for an ultrasound because, once again, they thought I had a lump. I was sitting in the waiting room and I called my mentor to tell him I was scared this time. He merely said, *"Rita, there's nothing there."* He did a Spiritual Mind Treatment. His words struck what Emma Curtis Hopkins would call a *"keynote"* within me.

I got off the phone as I was called into the ultrasound. During the procedure, all I could hear the doctor saying was, *"Are you sure they found something? There's nothing here."* He kept going over and over my breast with his equipment. There was nothing. He sent me home with a clean bill of health.

After that experience, I came to realize that I was done with this constant threat to my health and well-being. I was done with sitting on the edge of the doctor's table waiting for someone to tell me I was okay. I gave up my mother's disease and my grandmother's disease. I blessed them and told them I loved them, but that I was me and I was new in this moment. I no longer had a history of breast cancer. I knew that as I affirmed this, I was also clearing the way for my daughters and granddaughters. I even believed that I was clearing past generations of this belief in disease.

When I went for my next mammogram, I was told something pretty spectacular. I was told that my breasts were totally fatty tissue. They were perfect. They were no longer cystic.

You might ask why do I still go for mammograms even now? I do because I realize that, although I have faith in my health, I also know that there is a part of me that is still swimming in race consciousness. I will know when I have completely released that. When that time comes, I will do what is next.

I am grateful for health. I am grateful for doctors. I am grateful for anything that assists us in living full and loving and abundant health-filled lives. We work in tandem with medicine. However, what I do know is that there is a Power within each of us that will bring through us and to us whatever we believe. We will eventually come to realize that we are perfect health and we have always been perfect health. As Dr. Holmes wrote, "We believe the ultimate goal of life to be complete freedom from all discord of every nature, and that this goal is sure to be attained by all."

A new consciousness is rising, a shift is taking place. We are taking back our power. Through the consciousness of oneness, we will heal ourselves and our planet.

Affirmation:
I am free of all discord now.

40

Calling All Metaphysicians!

When an illness presents itself to a medical doctor, the doctor will approach the healing of that illness according to his or her field of study. One doctor may recommend surgery while another will use drug therapy. Another physician might say physical therapy is the answer. Each professional is looking for healing and there are many answers to the same question. All answers can offer solutions to the challenge.

The metaphysician deals with the challenge from one answer only and that is the unseen Principle, the world of Spirit, the mental cause. We do not contradict the medical world and we welcome its support for we know that, behind it all, Spirit works through and as everyone involved for the revealing of Truth to take place and healing to occur in the individual.

I bring this idea to the state of the world right now. As I read the headlines and the comments from many on Facebook and elsewhere, I see that everyone from presidents to citizens see a different solution to what they think ails the world. Everyone also has a different view on what ails the world. It seems that there is a great confusion as to what everyone wants as a whole. The country and the world is divided. Truth is hard to locate. Fear runs the show.

Instead of lashing out in anger and fear, the metaphysician goes deeply within for answers, realizing that the Universe in its true essence is harmonious, balanced, and whole. It is always seeking this state no matter what is occurring in the world of effects and conditions. It might be a battle of will against will, but beyond and behind it all, Spirit is seeking balance and wholeness. Sometimes this route can be long and seem tenuous. One thing for sure is that its outcome is secure.

The metaphysician in his/her laboratory begins to work in mind. The metaphysician can prove that spiritual thought force reigns supreme over material resistance. The metaphysician is called to action from a place of wholeness, harmony, and balance. The metaphysician sees that Divine Right Action is taking place in and through everyone and everything. What might seem terribly wrong is calling forth something completely right. Love does overcome the deepest fear and Light does cast out darkness.

Do not stand idly by. I invite all metaphysicians to go deep into their laboratories and continue their work. I invite all metaphysicians to reflect on the Power of the Unseen Principle of Love, Harmony and Balance and to call it forth, to live it each day. I invite all metaphysicians to contemplate the question: *What am I for?* I invite all metaphysicians to see from the heart and to continue to live from that place. I invite all metaphysicians to take loving, intelligent action. Love backed by faith, trust, and conviction moves the unseen in its direction unfailingly.

Affirmation:
I stand as a metaphysician backed by love and trust.

41

Thawing Out

Have you ever felt frozen? By frozen, I mean you can't go one way or the other. You are stuck in a decision or you know you should do something but you can't go all the way with it. I believe that frozen thoughts make frozen physical experiences. I believe that rigidity in thinking creates rigidity in the body.

I believe I must push into my life in order to experience it. I believe sometimes I hold back. Do you? Where are you frozen in your life? When I am experiencing tension and rigidity in my body, I know that it is caused by frozen areas of my life. The more I let go, the more the tension releases.

Fear is one of the biggest forces that freezes us. Fear of money, fear of health, fear of the world freezes all activity in our lives. If we are in fear, we cannot be in faith.

So how do we thaw? How do we release it all? There is a song by Rickie Byars that goes like this: "*I release and I let go. I let the Spirit run my life...*" It's easy to say, but do we, and how do we?

There is only one way I know to let the Spirit run my life. It is surrender. It is when I do not try to manipulate the outside world. It is when I discipline myself to think of love every time my mind is pulled in another direction. I do not believe this is something that we get to practice once. It takes lots of practice. I think we have to be vigilant keepers of our greatest treasure - our minds.

There is a Divine Intelligence within each of us moving, living, and breathing us. The more we surrender to it, the more our thoughts align with it. It is our true identity. It is all Power. One of my mantras now that I use any time I am confronted with anything is, "*God is all in all.*" It is all in all and that means it is all of me. In every moment it is awakening my cells, my mind, my heart to its Presence. It thaws every frozen place just by my recognition of it. There is nothing to hold on to. God's got me. It's got you. It's got all of us. God is always looking for an outlet. We have the choice to just let it flow fully through and as us.

Sunlight thaws the frozen ground just like the Light of Life Force/God thaws our hearts and minds. Wherever there is rigidity in my life, I let God flow through. What is God? God is correct thinking - love. God is all in all and all of me. It is all of you. It is a Presence of Love that turns to us as we turn to It. I'm thawing out just thinking of It.

Affirmation:
Wherever there is rigidity in my life, I let God flow through.

42

One Thing at a Time

Sometimes our lives can become overwhelming. We think we have to do everything at once. I love lists and setting priorities. I love the feeling of checking off tasks as I've completed them. Of course, there is always more to add to the list, but still, if I can see it on paper, it seems less daunting. If I keep it in my head, I feel overwhelmed.

I believe the same is true about things we want to change about our lives. It can seem overwhelming to look at everything and think we have to have it now. Suppose we want to improve our health, get out of debt, and find a partner all at once. We don't know where to start or what to do, so sometimes, we just give up.

What I have found that works for me is to focus on one thing at a time. When I do, as one thing improves, the improvement tends to create a ripple effect into another part of my life. Once I start the positive flow going, one step at a time, it cannot help in doing so.

This is because everything, in reality, is connected. We are not a bunch of parts working together. We are wholeness having different experiences. Wholeness cannot be divided. All of Rita is experiencing financial freedom and health at the same time.

So, I invite us today to make a goal list for our life and then pick one thing with which we'd like to start. Perhaps it is a relationship. We can give our positive intention and attention to it. We can change our thoughts about it. We can know we can make a difference. We can do one positive action to back up that intention. *Faith without works is dead*, and in order to prove the Principle, we must take action.

I believe as we begin with one thing at a time, a ripple effect does take place. It's so much easier to focus on one thing, and then another, and then another. As we apply Principle to our life, life gets better and better. Even when it seems to have gotten as good as it can get, there is still more. We are beings of light and love, forever expanding.

Affirmation:
Focusing on one thing at a time, I take action and my life expands.

43

Why Do Bad Things Happen to Good People?

There were two enormous earthquakes this week in different parts of the world. I'm sure living in those two places is quite stressful right now. My heart goes out to anyone who is suffering and, as many of us do, I ask the question, "*Why do bad things happen to good people?*" Why does a little child suffer or why does a mother or father die, leaving their children orphans? Why do bad things happen to good people?

There are a multitude of answers to this question and many religious leaders try to answer it to the best of their ability. That is our job, isn't it?

I have an answer and it is: *I don't really know.* I can only think about it and relate it to the Principle I believe in, and then come up with the best answer for me. However, in reality, *I do not know*. I can tell you what I have come to believe but that is just my belief. I think we each have to delve deeply into life and come up with our own answers to questions like these. We each have a Divine mind that holds all the Wisdom of the Universe within it. We can each feel truth when it comes from within our own hearts.

As I ponder this question, I come up with one thing that makes sense to me, according to Principle. Let me restate Principle first: Principle states that God is everything and that we live in a world of Cause and Effect. If this is the case, there are no good or bad people, and there is no good or bad. There are only people. There is only life. Challenges are experiences on the road of Divine Evolution and they present us all with opportunities to love each other and ourselves more. We are at choice all the time even if it appears we are not. Challenges present us with opportunities to raise our consciousness. Challenges call us to remember who we are when we have forgotten.

In the case of earthquakes such as these, I know there must be all sorts of opportunities to love and help and feel our oneness. Look what happened on the day of September 11, 2001. New York City and the world united their hearts in a huge way.

Ernest Holmes once wrote, "**The world will soon realize that it has learned all it can through suffering.**" He also wrote, "*Evil will cease when we stop believing in it.*" I believe this. I believe this time will come, perhaps right now. Maybe there are already some of us who know that we have learned all we can through suffering. I know that the times that I have suffered have been some of the most spiritual times in my life. Did I call these times to myself? I'm the only one who can answer that question.

As I watch and read the headlines and see how angry and divided people are, I do not wonder why Mother Nature also rumbles and roars. We are one and what is felt in the individual is felt everywhere. Am I blaming all of us for the earthquake? I am saying we are one, and I believe there is a ripple effect to everything. Again, I always look to Principle for my answers. It never fails me, even if I do not like the answer.

This is a Universe of order, not chaos. We are each individuals but also united in this Universe. There is no separation between us and the Universe. If we find ourselves in a challenge, instead of trying to find out what is wrong with us, why don't we instead look at it as a call to love more deeply. Mother Teresa was the best example of this as she walked through the pain and challenges on the streets of Calcutta and other places. She didn't see bad people suffering. She saw more reasons to love and awaken each person to their Divinity.

The only reason I can come up with for suffering is *separation*. When we feel separate from each other, we suffer. When we feel separate from the Divine Love, we suffer. There is a Law of Cause and Effect in place in each of our lives. We are governed by our use of it. It is impersonal.

Life is. There is no death. We are immortal. An earthquake cannot take away something that lives forever. I trust that all the people that are experiencing tragedy due to a natural disaster are infused with Love right now. I trust that their cries of despair are answered with more love and caring than they've ever experienced before. I trust that the Divine in each of them rises to the top of their individual crisis and fills every need. I trust that they are awakened to how amazing and powerful they are. I trust that suffering ends now!

There are no good or bad people. There are only Divine beings on the journey of the one Life that never ends. There are no good or bad things, there are only experiences that call out for us to love more—beginning with ourselves.

Affirmation:
I see through the veil where only love, compassion and understanding are present.

44

Just Change Your Homepage

I woke up this morning and opened my computer to do my morning ritual: meditation with Deepak Chopra and the writing of my blog. I was bombarded, as I usually am, by my homepage and all its negativity. I like to be informed, but it is amazing how enticing it can be to see a tab that says, *"You'll be amazed by these pictures of the Titanic,"* or some other headline that can easily suck you in. Of course, these are never positive headlines.

This morning I finally told myself I'd had enough. I have discipline. I can resist. I can just click on through to my blog, etc. I just hate seeing these images as the first thing in my morning.

Suddenly, I realized I could set my homepage. I don't know why I never thought of it before. Duh! So, I googled the instructions and did it. My homepage now is just a browser. If I want the news, I'll Google it. Otherwise, I can just wake up and go straight to my quiet meditation.

This experience brings up something for me. How many times are we confronted with experiences that seem like we do not have a choice? We believe we are at the mercy of something, some idea, or someone.

This is not true because the one thing that is certain is that we are beings of volition and choice. We are individualized expressions of the one Spirit with a conscious mind that is always at choice. If it were not true, we would be robots. Ignorance is not knowing this, and just moving through life as a victim of the choices of others.

We have dominion. We do not have dominion over another person's experience but we are at the helm of our own ship. The question might be *what is the cost of our choice?* Does it mean we will have to make a change in our life? Perhaps that change seems difficult or one that would take total trust and faith on our part.

Today, I took the initiative to either take in the negative or release it. It was as easy as changing my homepage. I believe that we can do this in any part of our lives. And, I believe that if we think it will be difficult, it will be. That is the way the Law works. It gives us our mental equivalent.

However, I also believe and know that this same Law will support us in our decision. It will open doors where there were once only walls. Life flows when we flow with it as beings of choice and volition. Our highest good is always right here. Spirit is always right where we are. As Ralph Waldo Emerson wrote, "*There is no big or small to the Soul that maketh all.*"

We are capable and supported in choosing what we want for our lives. It is a decision. We must take the leap, and then go out and live as if it were already true. It does take faith, but that is what living on this plane of action is all about. Growth through faith. And always with love. It can be as easy as just changing your homepage.

Affirmation:
I have the power to change my homepage when needed.

45

What You Seek is Seeking You!

Henry David Thoreau wrote, "*Many men go fishing their whole lives and find it was never fish they were after.*" I am resonating with this quote today. What do we want that we are disguising as something else in our quest to get it? I bring my attention to my own life.

It all began in 1998 when I embarked on the journey of embodying the Science of Mind Principles. I had experienced many different spiritual journeys in my life from being born a Catholic, to the hippie culture of the 60s, to practicing Mormonism, to Crystals and New Age, to being agnostic. It was the day I let go of everything that I truly began to realize that it wasn't religion I was after. It was a sense of peace and well-being.

Isn't this what we all want as human beings on this planet? Do we want to feel safe, to love and be loved, to feel we are not alone, and to feel we are part of something greater than what might be presenting itself in our lives? We might disguise all this in the form of different religions and ideologies and social clubs and groups and find ourselves fishing for the right one. However, when this longing is broken down, what I find is whatever I am looking for is right here where I am. I'm just not going to find it out there, and for that matter, it never was taken away and never can be taken away. As the Persian Poet, Rumi, wrote, "*What you seek is seeking you.*"

This is why I have embraced the Science of Mind Philosophy.

It never tried to sell me anything. It gave me the path back to myself. By studying it and practicing it, I have come to know that all that I could ever desire in the way of peace and love is right where I am. I have taken my own Power back, my own mind back, my own volition to live my life as I desire, knowing that I am equal to everything showing up. There is only Spirit, which is love, and a Law of Cause and Effect that is exact. This all resides within me and connects me to everything. What goes out must come back. I am on a journey of unfoldment and expansion.

I am open at the top which means that there is always more to learn; there is always more expansion; there is always an opening to more and more inspiration from within. I am open at the top of my crown chakra, the portal where I am connected to the Infinite space of Divine Energy that intuits through me, as me. We do not make energy, create it or give it to others; we open up to what is already here.

And so, I love living free of dogma. I love knowing that I have the freedom to fall and get back up again. I am grateful to feel the eternality of my soul. I am grateful to live in peace, knowing that if all structure was to fall away, the Truth would still exist. *I am a Spiritual Being living in a Spiritual Universe, governed by **my use** of the Law of Cause and Effect.*

Affirmation:
I am always free to start again.

46

Bold Love Unleashed

The famous words of John F. Kennedy echo in my mind this morning. "*My fellow Americans, ask not what your country can do for you, ask what you can do for your country.*" I ask this question in a different way. "*My fellow Divine Beings, ask not what God can do for you, ask what you can do for God.*"

When I use the word God, please remember, I am not referring to a man on a cloud somewhere. I am referring to the very Principle of Life that is my life and yours. God is moving through all of creation, a Divine Principle, creating from itself, as us, as the Universe. So, coming from this place, *ask not what God can do for you, ask what you can do for God.*

In answer to this question, what we can do for God is to express ourselves boldly and authentically. We can let God out. Another word for God, in the mind of the great transcendentalist Ralph Waldo Emerson is, "Love." God is Love. The greatest expression of God would be to be bold love unleashed.

Bold love unleashed is not afraid to live with passion. Bold love unleashed speaks its truth. Bold love unleashed shares itself authentically and fully. Bold love unleashed replaces fear with faith. Bold love unleashed is peace within the storm. Bold love unleashed has faith and trust in itself because it knows that the Power that created everything is behind its very breath. Bold love unleashed lives as integrity and stands by its word. Bold love unleashed knows that its word is Law and therefore always speaks its word with love. Bold love unleashed respects all life because all life is the life of God. Bold love unleashed has the audacity to say, "*I am God. I am Divine. I am you and you are me.*" Bold love unleashed believes in itself because it knows that it is a Divine expression of the Most High. In the words of Ernest Holmes, "*Whomever you are, be proud, you are a Divine idea in the mind of God.*"

Bold love unleashed takes responsibility for its life. When things look the worst, bold love unleashed knows that it is a co-creator of what is in front of it. If it is not serving the highest good, just as it was created, it can be uncreated and recreated. Bold love unleashed doesn't doubt its power because it knows that its power is the Power that keeps the stars in balance and the earth spinning. Bold love unleashed creates a life that is harmonious and peaceful because it **is** peace. It places no limits on Principle, and it lives free and focused on expressing Principle to the highest and best.

I am bold love unleashed and so are you. We are connected in one Field of Energy. It's up to each of us how much of that bold love we want to unleash. The more we unleash, the more bold and loving the Field is. As we ripple together, we create harmony and balance. That harmony is created by love, and love alone.

Affirmation:
I am bold love unleashed.

47

What Can I Do?

I wrote this during the COVID-19 pandemic in 2020 but I believe the message applies to all times of challenge.

I believe in our spiritual evolution and that we are being asked to practice resilience. We must go deeper into our own intuition. We must remain kind and compassionate. We must remain awake and alert. We must be smart and take care of ourselves. Most importantly, we must remember who we are.

I'll start with the idea of being resilient. During these times, frequently we are given new information. It is becoming even more imperative that we shift and change. Yesterday, for just a moment, I contemplated what morbidity felt like. STOP! We have a choice. We cannot go into fear. Instead, we must become creative in our approach to our lives. Instead of fighting what is, we must come up with new and creative ways to give our gifts to the world, to become helpers instead of fighters.

There is so much we can do. Consciousness is non-local, omnipresent. Even sitting in our own houses, we can use our minds to fill up the one Field we all share with love and affirmations. With the internet, phones, and computers, we can do so much more in the way of communicating our love. Be resilient!

We all have the gift of Intuition. It is God/Spirit/Intelligence within each of us knowing Itself. When we tap into this Mind, we will be guided and directed in just the right way. We will know when to stop and when to go. We will know how to promote safety for ourselves and others. We will know what is ours to do. Intuition is a gift that all of us have. However, we must take time to connect with it and allow it to move through us. It takes trust. It takes faith. It takes listening with an open mind and heart.

As the beautiful quote by Mr. Fred Rogers challenged us to *"look for the helpers"* in scary times what I know is that we are the helpers. Each of us is a helper and we must look for ways to help, to be kind, to be compassionate. It can be easy when stressed to react and separate even more from each other. Take a breath first and ask, *"What would compassion do here?"*

There is nothing more important than to remember who we are. We are not mere mortals being pushed around by the world of conditions. We are Divine Beings, Absolute Intelligence, Love Personified with all the faculties of God— Truth, Beauty, Power, Wisdom, Light, Joy, Peace, and Love. There is nothing we cannot do.

All of this will lead us back to ourselves. I take responsibility for worsening this virus anytime I further separate myself mentally and emotionally from others. I do not have to touch you or even see you to love you. You are my brother, my sister, and we are one.

My friend asked me to put a Spiritual Mind Treatment on Facebook that we could read should we need it or desire it. For those of you who do not know what a Treatment is, simply put, it is praying the solution to any challenge. It is recognizing that the Power and Presence of the Divine Spirit is always with us. Spiritual Mind Treatment moves energy and creates an avenue of Light within us, allowing our desires to manifest. It is spoken into the one Field of Energy, the one

Mind, the Law, and is felt everywhere.

So, here is what I know…

I recognize the Power and Presence of Spirit, God, Source as everywhere present. This Power is the only Power there is. It is pure, unlimited, eternal Energy and has never been touched by anything. It is just waiting for me to impress it with my Word.

I know that I am this Power, this Energy, this Source. I know this as me and as each person reading this. I know it as all of creation. We are the Power and the Presence of Spirit/Source/God beating in and as the same heartbeat called the Universe.

Knowing this is the Truth, I know there is nothing that we cannot do during this time of change and seeming challenge. I claim the revelation of love, harmony, balance, and good. I know that each and every one of us is Divinely guarded, protected, guided, and directed individually and collectively on this journey of light and love. Speaking this Truth, I know I am removing any obstacle to the demonstration of healing right here and now. I stay firm in this, knowing the Power and Presence of Love endures and is the healing Power. It is eternal, unstoppable, a Cosmic force "whose sweep is irresistible." It reveals itself now, everywhere through and as everyone. Love is. Light is. Healing is.

I sit in a well of gratitude for the demonstration of all I have written here – my Word. I give thanks for a clear consciousness of healing revealing itself in love right now. I give thanks for the oneness, the unity, the grace that manifests itself through all of creation. I give thanks for the healer in each of us and the healed. I give thanks for the perfect outcome for each of us in the perfect way, individually and collectively.

With my thanksgiving, I release my Word as Law, knowing it is already fulfilled. It is unstoppable. It transmutes everything into love now. And so it is!

Affirmation:
Love is. Light is. Healing is.

48

Everything Comes at a Price

Do you look at the price tags when you are shopping? I do. It's a habit. If I want a certain dress, I look at it and see if I think it is worth the price that is asked. Sometimes the answer is yes, and sometimes no. The other day, I paid $9 for a loaf of gluten-free bread. I later stated, I wouldn't buy that again. It wasn't worth it.

Something has changed for me and it is the idea of "*can I afford this?*" If I want something, truly want it and I believe I can have it, then I know in the heart of me that the Universe will pay that price tag, no matter what it is. However, I must have the mental equivalent of that price tag. My mental price tags are constantly growing.

I haven't always felt this way. I spent much of my early life looking at price tags with longing. I remember my mother waiting until Christmas Eve to buy our Christmas tree because the trees were cheaper. She had no reason to do that; her husband was a doctor. In fact, I always remember my mother as one who was frugal about everything. Perhaps, it is because she was a baby from the Depression era. I'm sure a little of that brushed off on me until I made the conscious choice to change my consciousness.

I wonder how many of us are always looking for the cheapest deal. I would be dishonest if I said I didn't do that, and yet, lately, I've been thinking about that, too. Why am I looking for the cheapest deal or trying to get the most out of a sale or service, and then in the same breath, saying I want people to pay me more for my service? It is a contradiction, and the truth is, what we reflect out into the world comes back to us. Life moves in circles and we receive what we give. If we are living our lives to just get by or to give the least amount, then that is our reflection. There is no two ways about it. Everything comes with a price, but the price is in mental coinage. I do not run out, rushing about, just spending money without the consciousness to back it. I know where my consciousness is and I must start right where I am and move it forward in degrees.

Yes, everything comes with a price and the price we pay is governed by our belief. Through quantum physics, we know that everything is always changing and shifting. It is our thoughts and feelings that bring back our desires to us and create our lives. Although we might try to change things in the 3-D world, if we want the change to be lasting, it must take place in the Field, or what we call the One Mind, Source, God. The many mystics have taught this for eons so it really is nothing new.

As Ernest Holmes wrote, "*We are immersed in an Infinite intelligence that receives the impress of our thought and acts upon it.*" When we come to understand and accept this one simple truth, our whole lives will change, for we will know that the place we need to work is in the unseen or the mental field. Please do not interpret what I am saying as all you need to do is sit on the couch and think good thoughts and make things appear out of thin air. What I am saying is I begin in the mental field and change my consciousness about whatever it is that I want to change in the material world. I must truly look at myself and why I think the way I do and then change the way I am thinking by changing my beliefs. I do this through Spiritual Mind Treatment, meditation, and using affirmations.

We are vibrating right now, and our vibration is all about our feeling moving out from us and bringing our intentions back to us at exactly the same level as our vibration. When I am angry, I meet anger. When I am in lack, I meet lack. When I am telling myself that I am unhealthy, I create more reasons to be unhealthy. We cannot escape the power of our consciousness.

For example, what if instead of thinking everything is going wrong in our lives or looking for the cheapest way to live our lives, we gave gratitude for all that we have and focused on everything that is going right. I know, through experience, that if we did just that, everything in our lives would shift for the better.

As I said, I have not always thought this way. In fact, I have lived rather unconsciously, blaming my outside conditions for the condition of my life. When I lived in Los Angeles there were lots of reasons to buy into the lack-consciousness of many of us who were actors. *It's hard to make it as an actor in Los Angeles* was one of our most popular ballads that we sang. And so it was. Here on Kaua`i, many of us talk on and on about how hard it is to find a house to rent or buy. And, so it is!

So, the first place to start is to remember who we are. We cannot progress any further than our self-concept. Loving ourselves always comes first. In *The Science of Mind*, Dr. Holmes tells of the practice of the early spiritual initiates who were told to cross their hands over their chests and repeat the mantra "*Wonderful, Wonderful me!*" It seems that the journey of self-love is as old as our planet is.

We can move energy in the direction of our choosing. We

can think greater thoughts and therefore have greater lives. We know beyond a shadow of a doubt that *it is done unto us as we believe*. However, sometimes we do not want to accept this because it puts all the responsibility on our shoulders.

I am sold on this idea of paying for my life in full, and not by compromise, but by thinking the highest and best for myself and living from that place. My mental coinage is always about self-worth.

Good comes with a price that must be paid with *mental coinage*. Yes, we must sacrifice our old ways of thinking. We can't pray for more money because just by doing so we are affirming that we do not have it. We can't pray for love, for praying for it is telling the Universe that we think that it is outside of ourselves.

When we can understand that we already have it all, we will see golden highways where there was once only dirt. We will know love, where we only felt loneliness.

Everything comes with the price of sacrificing our old worn-out belief system and replacing it with a belief in the Magnificence of our True Nature. It can feel quite expensive to give up everything we once believed in; however, the reward is equally expensive. We do not have to wait for the sale items to receive our good; there is enough for all of us and it is all here right where we are.

If we think this thought is too big to conceive right now, that's okay. Just start where you are and think a little higher every day. Push your envelope of consciousness. Give a little more out even if it is just a penny. Open up to receive a little more even if it is just finding a penny. The goal is expansion and we all have to start where we are. There is nothing to be ashamed of and everything to love about ourselves.

I love this journey and when I accept that it is an eternal one, it makes it even more fun. I am grateful that I know beyond a shadow of a doubt that I have the ability to change my consciousness and therefore change my life anytime I choose to do so.

Affirmation:
I pay the price for my life with a full consciousness of love.

49

Arising from the Story

"As my sufferings mounted, I soon realized that there were two ways in which I could respond to my situation – either to react with bitterness or seek to transform the suffering into a creative force. I decided to follow the latter course" (Martin Luther King Jr., via Mastin Kipp's The Daily Love).

Over the course of my life, I remember many times I had negative experiences where I immediately turned my suffering into a Creative Force. I remember one particular time when I was so devastated about an event that I went on to write a story in which I created the outcome of the event in the way I would have liked to have seen it happen. Several years later, the reverse scenario occurred with different characters. By flinging my suffering onto paper, I literally healed myself and lived anew.

So, what is this Creative Force that lies within us seeking expression? It is God itself, expressing itself through us. It is the very Essence, Source, and Energy that manifests itself individually through us. By taking our suffering and reaching within to the Creative Force, we become the Phoenix rising out of the ashes. There is nothing we cannot heal.

I am a healer, a teacher, and an artist. I meet many people upon my path, including myself, that sometimes cannot get past their suffering wound. Another word for the wound is our *story*; the story of *"you done me wrong,"* or an illness, or a financial disaster, loss of a loved one, or any tragedy. We have read about races of people who will not let go of tragedies that happened generations ago and continue to pass the anger and hatred on to the next generation and the next.

We are born with the tendency of the race within us. We can live this tendency or choose to transform the suffering into a creative force. Along with Martin Luther King, Jr., I am thinking of Elie Wiesel, Auschwitz survivor and author of dozens and dozens of books. Could there be a greater suffering than Dr. Wiesel's?

I have read about and witnessed survivors of severe abuse and violence come forward and reach within to the creative force. They have not only transformed their own lives but assisted in the transformation of thousands upon thousands of lives.

How many of us are still stuck in our stories, refusing to let go, wallowing in the story? Can we take our small, everyday sufferings and turn to the Power within us and use it for good?

It is time. We are living in the most powerful time of Spiritual transformation. We are coming out of thousands of years of darkness into the Light once again. Forgiveness, Resilience, Faith, Trust, and Surrender to the Creative Force within us is the key to transforming our lives, no matter what we have experienced. We are each an individualized expression of the Creative Force. Can we choose to use this Energy today for the transformation from dark to light?

Affirmation:
I am a light worker using my energy for good.

50

The Game of Life

In her book *The Game of Life*, Florence Scovel Shinn writes, *"Many people consider life a battle, but it is not a battle, it is a game. It is a game, however, which cannot be played successfully without the knowledge of the rules or Spiritual Law."*

Life is a game, but like every game, it has rules. The Spiritual Laws or rules that Florence Shinn is writing about is the "Law of Giving and Receiving." What we put out into the Universe most definitely comes back to us. We do not get to play the game of life and make up our own rules. There is a Law and it is exact and guaranteed.

For example, we cannot create abundance from lack consciousness. We cannot create health from claiming that we are always sick or by mentally succumbing to flu season. The most powerful among us Treats and moves their feet in the direction of their Treatment. If it's health we want, then we must claim health and act like a healthy person. We prepare ourselves mentally for what we do for our bodies physically, not the opposite.

Life is a game and it should be played like a game. If the goal is to win, then we have to play to win. If we use the Law of Giving and Receiving correctly, we will reap its gifts. We also have spiritual skills that we get to refine and use as we play the game of life: Perception, Intuition, Imagination, Vibration, Belief, Intellect, Decision – to name a few. Skills are necessary when playing any game. These are skills that must be used, refined, and corrected when needed.

Let me go through them quickly. Everything is perception. If we have a challenge and we change the way we look at it, the challenge will shift. I can look at a challenge in my life as an opportunity to learn more or dig deeper into my inner or spiritual self.

My intuition must be developed. If I hear the voice of intuition and ignore it, I will not reap its benefits. Intuition is not just something that is happenstance. It can be received on demand when I truly stop and listen to my inner voice.

My imagination is a powerful tool and it swings in many directions. I can envision what I want and I can also spend time envisioning what I don't want. That's called worry.

What about vibration? Am I vibrating at the frequency of what I say I want in my life? If I want to be more prosperous, then I have to act more prosperous. Holding onto every dollar is not prosperity consciousness. If I want to have more, I have to give more.

Belief holds everything in consciousness. I have deep beliefs that have been with me since I was a child. If they do not serve me, am I working on changing them? Sometimes I am surprised when a belief comes up that I thought I'd let go of long ago. I liken it to getting a hilahila weed out of my garden. It takes deep digging and sometimes I get pricked, but that doesn't stop me from digging deeper. In order to rid myself of the weed, I must dig out the tap root. This takes persistence.

Using my intellect constructively by learning new things keeps my mind fresh and open to new ideas that I might not have previously conceived. I am always reading, studying, and listening to powerful people speak and teach. I do my best to use my intellect intelligently. I choose what information I take in and what I discard.

My ability to make an irrevocable decision is paramount in getting anywhere in life. I have to be direct and state what it is I want. Then, I have to make a decision to act, to go for it, and to decide that my success is assured. Action has to follow our decisions.

Our Word is the greatest tool that we have and will be more powerful when all our skills are in place and working. I rely on this promise often and state it in my Treatments: "*My word shall not return unto me void, but shall accomplish that where unto it is sent*" (Isaiah 55:11).

Florence Shinn wrote, "*If one asks for success and prepares for failure, he will get the situation he has prepared for.*" How many times have we Treated or wanted something in our life, stated it, and then did everything to the contrary just in case it didn't happen? We cannot say one thing and act in another way.

We must be true to our Word. We must believe in our Word. We must trust the Law of Giving and Receiving. It's one thing to say we know there is a Law and another thing to believe in it, trust it, and use it.

Life is a Game and we are playing it. We might be playing with poor skills and feel that we are losing, but we are getting exactly what we put into the game. The Truth is that it all comes back to ourselves. We must know ourself as God, as all Powerful. We must love ourselves and treat ourselves with kindness and respect. We must trust ourselves, knowing that when we think, God is thinking. When we use our Word, God is speaking. This is not vanity; it is Truth.

The game can't be played from the outside in. We must get

into the inner workings of the game and play it from that place.

We are all potential winners in the Game of Life and there is no competition. When I adhere to the Law of Life and play the game, respecting that law, life ceases to be a battle. Instead, it becomes a wonderful adventure. When I am on the adventure of life, playing the game with all my skills and sharpening those skills on a daily basis, I meet success around every corner, even the unexpected corners. When you are open and ready, you might be surprised how your good shows up.

Affirmation:
I am a winner at the Game of Life.

51

You've Got a Great Life

I was on the phone with someone who had never been to Hawai`i, and right before hanging up, he said, "*You two* (my husband and I) *got the great life over there.*" He was referring to our life here on the beautiful island of Kaua`i. Interestingly, I immediately let him know (jokingly) that we weren't just sitting here sipping Mai Tais, and that we were working hard. This answer did not necessarily have to be spoken to my friend, but the deeper answer here is revealed to me.

I do have a great life. However, what I know is that I co-created this life with the Law of my Being. My energy is equal to this life. I took a long time getting here and had many detours along the way. However, each detour was perfect and led me here to this "great life."

Sometimes we are afraid to make decisions. We think that if we do not make the right decision, all is lost and we will never succeed. We think that every decision has to be the perfect one. What I know from my own experience of many, many years is there are no mistakes and the only important thing is to MAKE A DECISION.

Decision-making is not an analytical process where you get to write down all the possible pros and cons. Pros and cons are written from past experience and, "*Principle is not bound by precedent,*" according to New Thought author, Thomas Troward. Decisions come from the present moment and are born out of our Cosmic Urge to express life. When we are in touch with that Identity and our rightful place as Cosmic beings and Cosmic creators, our decisions reflect this. I know this, because I have not always made decisions from this Cosmic place. I have moved my life forward somewhat unconsciously.

Thank God for what I call "Grace," because even when I fell, the Universe caught me. I might have experienced emotional bumps and bruises, but again, there are no mistakes. There are only lessons.

Yes, I have a great life, but I am equal to it. We all have the opportunity to have a great life. It is just a matter of getting in touch with the highest part of ourselves, the passionate side of ourselves, the urge that calls us into expression that is always led by love. It isn't always easy to hear it and follow it. Sometimes, we have to take all those detours and side roads, but that is okay. We will all eventually come home. The statement used by many, *"Life is a journey, not a destination"* is a very true statement.

The next time someone tells me how great my life is, I will let them know that their life is great also and that they have every opportunity I have to express that great life. Enjoy your great life, everyone!

Affirmation:
My life IS great.

52

My Mental Rehearsal

We are studying the book, *You Are the Placebo*, by Dr. Joe Dispenza. It is a book that is awakening me to my Power in an even deeper way. This week, we discussed the transforming effect of a technique called "Mental Rehearsal." Experiments have proven that when you mentally rehearse a skill you want to attain or a goal you want to reach with enough feeling and emotion, you will change your chemistry and bring forth the manifestation of that which you have mentally rehearsed.

Mental rehearsal is not a new concept and it can be used to our advantage or disadvantage. I remember mentally rehearsing my failures many times. At the time, I didn't realize that was what I was doing. I was unconscious of my Power. For example, when I was an actor on my way to the audition, I sometimes mentally rehearsed everything that could go wrong, including forgetting my lines. And so it was! You get the point. I think we can all think of times when we unconsciously rehearsed our failures. Well, if we've proven we are good at mentally rehearsing our failures, now we get to turn it all around.

Today when I mentally rehearse, I am conscious that I am in a Powerful process. I am careful when I mentally rehearse. Whether it is going to the doctor for a test for my health, or when I am about to give a talk at my Center, or when I'm getting ready for an important meeting with someone, I mentally rehearse my success.

We already know that something neurochemically happens

when we are mentally and emotionally involved with an idea. When we are passionate and filled with excitement and love, we are sending out strong signals to the Universe. It has to come back to us. It's science.

I invite us to begin to consciously mentally rehearse our success. I invite us to mentally rehearse how we want to live in our world and how we want to bless our world. If we can be disciplined about it, we can succeed. It's already been proven. Others have done it, and if we look at our life, we'll see we've already done it. Let us consciously do it now. By changing our mind, we are changing the world.

Affirmation:
I mentally rehearse my life of abundance,
love and health.

53

I Tithe Because I Can

Yesterday, my husband and I had a discussion about the Law of Tithing. We practice it and it is one of the most important and necessary practices in my life. If you don't know what it is, it is the practice of giving 10% of your gross earnings to someone or some organization that spiritually nourishes you. It's about giving back to the Universe/God first. It's called a Law because, like the many Spiritual Laws of the Universe, it is scientific and provable. Like the Law of Gravity, it always works.

I first learned about tithing when I was a Mormon. I did it with blind faith and didn't know exactly what I was gaining from it. I did it because someone told me to do it. However, I can say that there wasn't a time during that period when I was in want of anything. All my needs were always met. There was never a bill I couldn't pay or expense I couldn't meet.

After I left the Mormon Church (another story for another time), I fell into just "doing." I was raising children, but I was also having a lot of fun with life. I didn't tithe during that period because I hadn't really learned what the Law of Tithing was truly about. I didn't have prosperous thinking. I would say I was living unconsciously, looking only to earn money and spend it fast.

As time passed and my life changed drastically, I found myself at a Church of Religious Science. I was in one of the lowest financial times in my life. This lasted for well over ten years. I struggled financially. I was in deep debt. I donated to my Church, but I only gave what I thought I could give - $5 here, $2 there, and sometimes as much as $10. I still didn't understand tithing or the Law of Circulation. I was holding onto every penny that came into my life.

Then, one day I went to a workshop taught by Edwene Gaines, a Unity minister who dedicated her life to teaching people about the Laws of Prosperity. She challenged me to tithe, really tithe, to give 10% of everything I made to someone or some organization that spiritually nourished me. She dared me to do it and to trust that I would prosper because of it. I accepted her challenge because after she told her own story, something inside of me said, "Why not me?" Again, I was deeply discouraged about my ability to earn money in those days.

Still, I didn't know why I was tithing. I just did it in faith. I began to bring myself to a higher state of financial consciousness. One day one of my spiritual teachers asked the question of our class, "Why do we tithe?" We all gave answers, but she wasn't happy with any of them. She stated, "We tithe because we can." A light went on for me and I finally understood.

Yes, I tithe because I can. I can because there is always enough and more coming in. I do not have to hoard anything. Tithing frees me from lack consciousness. As I continued to tithe, something truly shifted in my consciousness. I never feared money again. I totally knew that I would always be taken care of. I didn't expect anything in return for tithing, but I knew that I always had plenty in my life. It wasn't blind faith; I was actually proving it because my life began to show it. I released myself from an enormous debt while tithing. I was not just physically debt-free but mentally debt-free.

When we began our Center for Spiritual Living, we created bylaws stating we would give 10% of our gross income in tithing to those who spiritually nurtured our Center or the world. We have never given up this practice, nor will we. We've been advised against tithing, just as I was advised to stop tithing when I was paying off my personal debt. We stick to tithing no matter what. Our Center has no debt and continues to flourish.

The Law of Tithing is not always about giving to those who spiritually nourish you. It could be a waitress who lifts your day by giving you extra wonderful service. It could be an organization that enriches you spiritually, emotionally, mentally. Tithing is giving back to your Source in the form of those who walk the earth plane with you.

As far as my financial affairs are concerned, tithing is the most important thing in my life. I trust this Law. It gives me peace of mind and I know it is perfect. I am grateful to tithe and I always love it when I have a surprise increase in income because I get to give more. I've lost all my fear of money and I am its master. It is my servant. As I increase my abundance consciousness, I expand my life. Tithing is one of the necessary steps to creating the life I want to live. I invite you to read more about the Law of Tithing, also called the Law of Circulation or Giving and Receiving, and I invite you to begin to practice it. Don't do it because I told you to; do it because you are ready for a shift in your life.

Affirmation:
As I give, I receive.

54

I Double Dare You

The term "double dare" has different definitions. The one I choose to use for the sake of this blog is "a challenge that is harder or naughtier than a regular dare." Now, I'm not going to dare you to do anything naughty, but I am going to continue to dare you and myself to live our lives in a more profound and deeper way. I think it is necessary because of the challenges of the world right now. It is daring just to remain positive with all that is bombarding us: unprecedented floods and storms, war and conflict, the next new COVID variant, travel restrictions, economic upheaval, climate change, and more.

I double dare you to trust amidst it all. I double dare you to believe in something greater than what you see. I double dare you to take your place among the great mystics and spiritual leaders of our world: Gandhi, Martin Luther King, Jr. Jesus, Buddha, Mandela. I double dare you to take your place among the people who changed our world in the way of science and invention: Einstein, the Wright Brothers, Bell, Hawking, Jobs, and so many more.

You might say to me, "But, I am not as great as they are. They have more intelligence than me. They are more courageous!" This is not a valid excuse. All men and women are truly created equal. We all have the same Power. We might not have been born into the same circumstances, but we have the same Power. And we can't use circumstances as an excuse either. Many have raised themselves up out of lowly circumstances. We all have the same Power.

The reason some of us succeed at life and others do not all boils down to one thing. It is the ability to make a decision to do so. The Power answers yes to our decision and our ability to walk persistently as if our decision is a reality. Whether it is the decision to be the best mother or the decision to invent a rocket to the moon, it takes definite decision, persistence, and the ability to see beyond what is.

I need to step back for a moment and define what I mean by "the Power." There is only one Power. It is called by many names: God, the Field, Jesus, Allah, Source. It is the Principle of Life that moves through all of creation. It is Invisible Energy and it is always vibrating and moving and waiting to take form. It has to take form because that is what it does. It is a Cosmic Force. It is you and me. Its ability is infinite, inexhaustible, omnipresent, and all-knowing. I love calling it "Divine Infinite Intelligence."

So, I double dare you to take your place with the definite knowing that you are this Power and have the power to transform yourself into whatever it is you set out to be. There will be obstacles. There will be times of seeming failure. There will be twists and turns. There will be advances and there will be times to remain quiet and still right where you are. However, the trust we have within us to stay steady and persistent is always our choice. I double dare you to live this way, always in love, always expressing in that highest state of consciousness.

I share this Ernest Holmes quote with you. I'm sharing it because it really states what we must do at times like these and how much belief we must have. I double dare you to live this challenge.

"Begin to blot out immediately, one by one, all false beliefs that man is limited, poor or miserable. Refuse

*to think of failure or to doubt your own power.
See only what you wish to experience and look at
nothing else. We are relieved of all thought of clinging
to anybody or anything. Cannot the great Principle
of Life create all for us that we need? The Universe is
inexhaustible. It is limitless, knows no bounds and
has no confines. We are not dependent on a reed
shaken by the wind, but on the Great Principle of
Life Itself for all that we need or shall ever have. It is
not some Power or a Great Power, but ALL POWER.
All we have to do is believe, never wavering, no
matter what happens. As we do this, we shall find
things are steadily coming our way and they are
coming without that awful effort which destroys the
peace of mind of the majority of the race. We know
there is no failure in God's mind and this is the Mind
on which we are depending" (The Science of Mind:
302).*

Affirmation:

I double dare myself to live my greatness.

55

How is Not a Good Question

"If you can hold it in your mind, you can hold it in your hand." These are the words of Bob Proctor, motivational coach, who writes and speaks of this principle in many of his presentations. In the Science of Mind and Spirit philosophy, we teach that it is the "Will" that holds our thought in place, allowing us to shift our consciousness and demonstrate in the world of form those experiences that we desire. Please do not confuse this with willpower. We do not **will** things to happen. However, the Will, or our ability to keep our thoughts clear and aligned, is ours to use. It is a powerful tool.

Many of us want to have better lives. We might want more abundance of finances. We might want to be better at having relationships. Maybe we want to be more creative in our work. We want to be healthy, strong, and vibrant. All the things we desire are possibilities if we are willing to accept and receive them. This means we must open up our consciousness of acceptance and allow the Law of Mind in Action to work through us.

The Law of Mind in Action is simply the magnifying vibration of the Universe that brings our desires toward us or pushes them away from us. It works all the time. It is vibrating as we are vibrating. It is attracting those experiences to us that match our vibration. We know now through science what the mystics have taught for centuries. It is all about vibration and it is done unto us as we believe.

It might seem too simple or too good to be true, but it's not. As simple as it is, it might be the most difficult practice to instill in our minds because we have been conditioned by outside causes for so long. As the author Neville Goddard put it, *"Man's chief illusion is his conviction that there are causes outside of himself."*

So, right now, can we bring something we truly desire to experience to mind? Then, with our Will, can we keep our thoughts stayed on it already being here? Can we act as if it were so? And, can we stop asking *"How will this happen?"* This question will stop everything. It will stop everything, because we will be getting in the way of a Power (The Law of Mind in Action) that doesn't know how it will happen and only knows that it is already happening. It is arranging the pieces of our demonstration in the way of people, experiences, and more.

Please do not confuse this with sitting on the couch doing nothing and just having good thoughts. Your only job is to walk as if it were already so, doing your part, following your intuition, daily disciplining your mind to think only of that which you want.

I will give you a simple example of the miracle of creation. Almost a decade ago, when we set the date to have our first Sunday Celebration Service here on Kaua`i, we did not have a venue. However, we did all of the above. We walked as if it were so, sending out announcements and following all leads that came to us. We knew it was already so. Within a short period, and well ahead of our schedule, we walked into a hotel and met a woman who totally embraced us and our Center and gave us a space for a fee that was unheard of on this island. The next day she left that hotel to work somewhere else. We were secured in our contract and went on to have our first service right on schedule.

"How" is not a good question in the formula of demonstrating our desires. Stay away from this question. Only use your analytical mind to do what is yours to do. Stay in your right brain, your creative brain, with unlimited possibilities for every moment and watch what unfolds. It will seem like a miracle but it is the natural order of the Universe.

Affirmation:
I walk into life as if my prayer is already answered.

57

A Difficult Beginning

During uncertain times, it is easy to feel that the life we once knew is unraveling. I am grateful we took the opportunity to travel to the mainland and visit family. I am grateful that we stepped beyond hesitancy and moved in the direction of our intentions to experience love and connection. Our trip was blessed and the connections are stronger because of it. So now what?

We returned to an island that is experiencing all sorts of feelings and consciousness; some of it based in fear. Our number of COVID-19 cases are higher than past statistics and the restrictions seem to be back again. Being a faith-based organization, we escape some of those restrictions, but still the fear in some of our congregation is still there. Our Sacred Journey is opening on October 8, and yesterday, we had three cancellations due to fear of traveling. I accept and respect where everyone's consciousness is. We must follow our own intuition and guidance.

I've already had COVID-19 and moved through it with ease and grace. I am deeply sorry for all who have not had the experience I had with it. I know it is real and that we must practice healthy choices in all our endeavors. However, I know something beyond this. I will not allow COVID-19 to stop the forward movement of my life.

There is something to be gleaned from all this. I believe that gleaning includes going deeply within and trusting the Power that is within each of us, the connection of love that moves through us, the intuition that guides us, and the possibilities of joy that are ours when we walk through our fears into our highest intention for our lives. As I said, I am so grateful that I walked through my fear and had the amazing connection with family and loved ones on the mainland. It was well worth it.

Bob Proctor, motivational speaker and author, talks about something called the "terror barriers." It is that fear that comes up when we make a decision for change and all the obstacles of consciousness - inadequacy, lack of funds, lack of time, and a million other hurdles rise up within us, forcing us back into complacency. Is that what is happening for many of us now? Is COVID-19 and all its variants creating a fear barrier within us causing us to retreat from the changes and advancements we want to make for our lives?

If so, it is time to stop resisting what is happening in the relative world and to seek inner guidance of how to walk through it to our higher purpose. There are opportunities presented right now for each of us. We cannot see them through clouds of fear. Vincent Van Gogh wrote *"The beginning is perhaps more difficult than anything else; but keep heart, it will all turn out all right."* I believe we are at the beginning of a great change in our world and the beginning is difficult. I believe that is what we are experiencing right now and if we persist in trying to keep things the same, desperately trying to go back to what was, we will not be privy to the amazing new world of advanced consciousness that is opening up right now. What is that changed world? It is us, using our innate Power to become greater, more loving, more connected, more abundant, more creative beings. We have to think outside of the box now. We have to love more, give more, and act more deliberately from a beginner's consciousness.

Affirmation:
I am free and powerful in a brand new world of consciousness.

57

Our Chief Illusion

Empowerment coach, teacher, author, and motivational speaker, Bob Proctor, spoke these words of Neville Goddard, *"Man's chief delusion is his conviction that there are causes outside of his own consciousness."*

I agree and I know and believe that this is more than an idea. It can be proven. Our Consciousness is everything. It will change our experience because we will change our relationship to the experience. Our perception is governed by our Consciousness. Contrary to this belief is a consciousness of victimhood where we believe that everyone and everything did it to us. One belief empowers us to be a vehicle for change and the other weakens us and leaves us at the mercy of the world of conditions. In fact, we are actually contributing to the negativity in the magnetic field. Ernest Holmes reminds us, *"One alone in Consciousness with the Infinite constitutes a complete majority."*

In *Science of Mind*, Holmes also writes, *"We believe that the ultimate goal of life to be a complete freedom from all discord of every nature and that this goal will be attained by all."*

This is important to me because I understand it is not about walking a tight rope and avoiding "bad things" happening to us. It is about experiencing whatever situation we are in as an opportunity to grow, expand, and reveal more of our power as creative spiritual beings. This is a freedom from discord. During the times that I have experienced difficulties, I have found the secret of digging deeper into my capabilities and intuition. Discord shifts to opportunity.

So, we have a choice during these challenging times. We can continue to blame everyone else for our world and resist what is, or we can embrace the opportunities for shift and change and, instead, be a positive force of love in the world. As I have stated before, we will do more good for the world by changing ourselves than by trying to fix the world. All the great contributions to our species have come from people who had a greater Consciousness than what had been thought to have existed up to that point. Think of all the great inventors, scientists, and spiritual leaders of change in our history.

If we can release ourselves from fear and open up to our calling and purpose instead, there are many opportunities here and now in the shift that is taking place. These times require people who are led by love, intuition, kindness, imagination, and more. Do you feel the call? I do.

Affirmation:
I am called to greatness and I answer yes.

58

How to Think

In the Science of Mind and Spirit, we do not teach people what to think; we teach them how to think. There is a big difference between the words *what* and *how*. One is dogmatic and the other is freedom.

For example, I will use my experience during the past two weeks of testing positive for COVID-19. How did I get through it by thinking from a place of healing? I let my thoughts of healing be my prevalent consciousness. I trusted that my body was responding to the knowing of my natural state of wholeness and health. I didn't think about specific things or ways of getting better. I let intuition be my guide. I let what I believe to be the perfection of the healing process to run its course. That process is always led by Love.

The Science of Mind is a philosophy of freedom. We know we are free to choose how we live our lives. We know that we are not being punished by an outside Power, but as we make choices, we either benefit or suffer from the consequences of those choices. It's called Cause and Effect. The Law of Mind in Action is a Law of Liberty, but not of license. We don't just get to do whatever we want. We have to answer to our choices. We also know that we are always causing effect and that we can change our circumstances by changing the Cause. Because we are the Cause, we have the freedom to change that Cause anytime we decide to do so. The only way to change Cause is to change our beliefs and perceptions about what is occurring in our lives.

The Science of Mind and Spirit is what I consider to be a beautiful philosophy that teaches Oneness and Love. It stays out of people's lives and their choices and merely creates an open space for healing and expansion. It leads people back to themselves and their Divinity. It gives us a way to deal with the challenges of living this earthly life by realizing that Spirit is the beginning of everything. Spirit or God or Source is more Powerful than anything else. It is Love, and no matter what, there is nothing more powerful than Love.

Affirmation:

I only think from the highest place of love.

59

Water Lily Magic

On our 20th Wedding Anniversary, as part of our celebration, we bought ourselves a water lily plant. I'd never had one before and my training in caring for it was minimal. All I knew about the lily was to place it in my water garden with at least five hours of sun, feed it once a month, and ultimately, to enjoy its blossom. I marveled at how it closed its bloom as dusk approached and then opened again the next morning with the sun. There is something so magical about water lilies. No wonder they were an obsession of the painter, Claude Monet.

So, for three days, I just marveled at my water lily plant and its one blossom until I woke up to find it sinking into the water. I had no idea what was happening and thought for sure I'd done something wrong with my care. I tried to lift it back out of the water and balance it between the lily pads. However, it just kept sinking. I finally realized I could go to Google to find out what was going on and hopefully repair my damage.

What did I find out? Simply, what any avid water gardener would already know; this is the way water lilies die. They slowly sink into the pond. The directions suggested clipping the dying bloom back with my finger nails. So, I did. I almost felt like I was ending a life. I couldn't just throw the bloom away, so I composted it with one of my other plants. I was sad to see my water garden blossomless. I wasn't sure what was next. However, the very next day, a new blossom began to show itself from under the water. What a miracle!

The mystics have always told us to look to Nature for our answers to life. Nature holds all the wisdom we could ever require. I am allowing the water lily to teach me. I even now trust the process of life on a deeper level. Nothing ever dies. Eternal life is like the water lily plant that just keeps giving of itself through the process of re-creation. There is a seeming death but there is no ending. The plant is still very much alive and giving birth again and again. The blossom is like our earthly body but our Spirit is like the plant, eternal.

I also learned that when we do not understand something, we might jump to the wrong conclusions. Many of us do not totally understand death, for example. Just because we cannot see something with our earthly eyes doesn't mean it is not there. Perhaps, we need to learn to feel more and see less. Our 5th dimensional senses are far greater than our finite 3-D world perception. Just as there is a lot more going on with my water lily under the water, blocked from my view, so it is with the Unseen world of Spirit.

Nature knows exactly how to take care of itself and all of Nature is unique and magical. A water lily's care is not the same as a daffodil's care. We are Nature and just as magical. We are all different and need different care. We know exactly how to take care of ourselves spiritually, mentally, emotionally, and physically. We should trust our intuition which is the same as instinct in Nature.

The greatest Mystic and Master Teacher, Jesus, once said, *"Judge not according to appearances, but by right judgment..."* Everything is not as it appears. For instance, you might be at the worst time in your life, feeling like you are sinking under that water like my water lily blossom. But it might just be that a part of yourself needs to die so the real you, the new you, can be born. What's weighing you down? Let it go and let the new be born. There is always a new blossom in the thing called your Life.

Affirmation:
I allow my life to blossom anew.

60

The Cosmic Dancer

I am in the process of writing my memoir and it has been eye-opening for me. In hindsight, I can see the times where I totally danced with the Cosmos and the times when I held myself back, resisted, and stumbled. Interestingly, those times of dancing in union with the Cosmos weren't necessarily times I was accepted by society for my choices but my step was perfect and my life flowed in rhythm.

Have you ever danced with a really good dancer? You don't even know the steps and that person will make you feel like Ginger Rogers, or for those of you a little younger, like you are on *Dancing with the Stars*, perfectly rehearsed and flowing your way to first place. This is a perfect metaphor for dancing with the Cosmos.

Let me give an example. There was a time when I was truly struggling with money. I could not make ends meet and, as the end of the month approached and the first of the month loomed in front of me, my nights became a series of rapid heartbeats, hot flashes of panic, and fears the first of the month would find me behind in my rent. However, with my 12th hour mentality, something always came forward to assist and usually I made it by the skin of my teeth. This pattern repeated in my life for several years while, at the same time, I sank into debt.

Then one day, when enough was enough, I shifted my actions, took full responsibility for my dilemma, and turned to the Cosmos for assistance. I began to dance with the Spiritual Laws of Tithing and Giving and Receiving. I opened up the channels of my own ability to receive. I began to realize how important it was to forgive myself and to feel worthy of good. I saw clearly that, up to this point, I had been jumping ahead of myself. I wanted it all, but I wasn't ready to receive it all, nor did I trust the Cosmos to deliver. I had to straighten out my thinking and my actions. I had to give over to the Power greater than me.

What I came to understand is that there is a Power, not just any Power, but one Power. I call it God, Universe and, yes, the Cosmos. It is Law and Order; it is Love; it is Flow. When you place yourself in its path by placing your consciousness in its flow, your life proceeds effortlessly.

What does Cosmos mean? It is defined as "the universe seen as a well-ordered and harmonious whole." When you look into the heavens or think upon the order and harmony of Nature, you will see that there is a Power that holds everything together in perfect equilibrium. Everything balances everything else; life ebbs and flows in order to move life forward. Even a forest fire is part of the order of the Cosmos. I invite you to look to Nature for the understanding of true collaboration and harmony, and then to imitate it. Give, receive, be your true self. You can't be a peach if you are a pear. Be the best pear and leave the peaches to be their best.

We are this Cosmos, this Universe. It resides in every cell of our bodies. We might think we are running our own show, but there is always something that sings and sings within us that is moving us to get in step and create harmony in our lives. It takes trust, a leap of faith, and perhaps, a bit of cha-cha-cha on our behalf. In other words, sometimes it feels like we are taking one step forward and two steps back.

Trusting the harmony of the Cosmos in our lives means

that when we are struggling or things are not moving as we would like them to, we are being signaled to take a breath and surrender to this Power and allow it to dance with us without hindering its step. We are being invited to allow it to take the lead.

In Hawai`i, there is a native dance called hula. When you witness a dancer truly performing this dance with perfection, you witness someone dancing with the Cosmos, flowing, and moving with ease and grace. It is a spectacular example, a metaphor for what life can be like when we surrender to the Cosmic Power that flows through all of creation. One might ask, "Where can I start? I don't know how to dance. I want my life to be easier. I just don't know how." Here's a way to begin.

Wherever you are in your journey, take a deep breath. Take full responsibility for what is happening in your life right now. Take another deep breath. Let go and forgive everything. Know that guidance and direction is right where you are. Claim that all the support required shows itself to you now. Take another deep breath. Let go and begin to move with the path of least resistance. If you hit a wall, breathe again. The wall is only signaling that a change in consciousness is needed. Take another deep breath and claim "I am worthy of a life filled with peace and joy." If something comes up again that whispers "No you are not; look what you've done in the past. You'll never do this," simply turn away from that thought, lovingly, while telling it that you do not think that way anymore. "I am the Universe. It dances with me. It guides and directs my path. I am safe right now. There is good for me and I claim it now. I am guided now. I walk in faith."

Then you have to act as if it were true even when it feels that it isn't. Each of these steps can be a process, so be gentle with yourself. Keep on believing in that Cosmic flow as your life. I know this method works for I have proven it to myself over and over again. To dance with the Cosmos, I must turn my control over to the Greater Dancer that resides within me, merge with it, and dance as one.

Affirmation:

I dance in the unlimited Cosmic Flow of life.

61

Who's Your Daddy?

When I volunteered in the California Prison system as a labyrinth and workshop facilitator, I had a friend who was the Director of Arts in Corrections. She possessed a lot of spiritual wisdom. Whenever I voiced any worry or concern about anything, she'd ask, with a twinkle in her eye, "*Who's your Daddy?*" In an instant, I'd be back on Principle, remembering I was always guided, guarded, and protected by the Power within me, my true Father in the Heaven within.

Edwene Gaines, a Unity Minister who focuses her ministry on prosperity, was challenged by someone when trying to launch her business, "*How will you ever acquire the funds for that?*" In the world of form it was true, she didn't have any money. However, she wasn't going to give into the lack consciousness that surrounded her. She simply said, "*I have a rich father.*" The person challenging her took her literally and was very impressed with her answer and let her know that she was very fortunate. Little did he know that Edwene had faith in the Power and Presence of God's abundance that was always there for her. Edwene Gaines went on to create a prosperous life helping others to do the same.

If we are feeling anything is too big for us to handle or too impossible for success, I would ask, "*Really? Who's your Daddy?*" Your answer to that question will hold within it the seeds for success or failure. Can we trust the Power of the Universe of which Ralph Waldo Emerson wrote, "*There is no big or small to the Mind which maketh all.*"

There have been many times in my life where I was trapped in the world of conditions, not finding the answer to my financial dilemmas. I didn't know about this Power within me, my True Identity. My life was very similar to Jesus' parable of the Prodigal Son. I had strayed far from the Truth of my being. I was trying to do it all on my own. I had even rejected the words of my earthly father who taught me through example, that yes, I could have anything to which I set my mind. All those years, I didn't necessarily know any better and thought I was doing the best I could. I was doing the best I could at the time but I did not know there was so much more and a much easier life for me.

So, in 1998, when I discovered the teaching of the Science of Mind, like a prodigal daughter, I came home. At first, I didn't realize all that was available for me. I felt guilty about so many things in my past and was far from forgiving myself. I struggled for probably the first five years that I was in this teaching. And then finally, something began to happen to me. I learned about truly feeling worthy to have the good that I sought. I was worthy to be happy, to be prosperous, to spend my life doing what I was called to do, and to know that I was always provided for. I started on the trek home. My real Daddy is Spirit. I am born of Divinity. I am a queen. My very DNA is Divine. I don't have to prove this anymore. This is now proven by science. There is something about me and you that is so much more than meets the eye. As the Master Jesus said, *"Judge not by appearances, but by right judgment."*

I am a prodigal daughter and I feel like I keep coming home again and again. Every time I am challenged to grow, I have to remember my Divine Heritage, my unlimited capabilities, and the Power within me that flows without obstructions, if I open up to that flow.

In the story of the Prodigal Son, the first son traveled off into the world and apparently wasted the wealth his father had given him. This signifies that part within us that thinks that our good can run out; that there isn't an unlimited Source that can never run out. The stay-at-home son in the story is like us too. He is the one who was home all the time but didn't recognize the good that was right in front of him.

The beautiful part of this story is the answer that it gives about who God is. God is Love. It doesn't judge. It doesn't care about our past. It is always here just waiting for us to come home. This is a comforting thought to me and I accept it as the Truth for all of us. God stands at the door of our mind just waiting for us to turn to It and allow the love to pour through. God is the very breath that breathes us with plenty and more to give and receive. God never left us. God is right where we are, always. This is because we are God. We can leave this knowing, this state of mind, but we can't leave ourselves. God expresses as we are and can only work by working through our consciousness.

Ernest Holmes once wrote, *"Prayer does something to the mind of the one praying. It does not do anything to God."* He also wrote, *"Individuality must be spontaneous; it can never be automatic. The seed of freedom must be planted in the innermost being of humanity, but, like the Prodigal Son, we must make the great discovery for ourselves"* (Science of Mind:25).

When we pray, or do Spiritual Mind Treatment, we open up our energy to recognize that God or Life Force is right here where we are, always supplying us. Whatever we require is only a realization away, an embodiment of this knowing in our subconscious so that it no longer argues with the conscious mind. This is scientific. This is a conscious effort, a spontaneous effort, a choice.

However, sometimes we get discouraged because it doesn't always happen all at once. But really, think about it. Do you realize how many years some of us have been thinking the opposite way? Please give yourself a break and take it easy. It does come. I am proof of it.

When we feel the current of self-love within us, when we can realize that there is nothing ever to forgive, that we were always doing the best we could, that we always deserved everything good; we will have come home; we will have arrived at the greatest party ever. Whether we do it here or after this life, or in the next life, or the next, or whatever you believe about eternity, we will all be at the party eventually. No one can ever be lost.

In the story of the Prodigal son, the father gives the wayward son a "seamless robe." What does it mean to be seamless? It means there is no beginning and no end. It means that there is no separation. It is one robe of Unity, total and complete Unity with the Universe, God, Life, Love. In fact, it is our destination, and it is right here already.

Let us get on with the party. How about you open your invitation right now?

Affirmation:
All the goodness of life has always been mine. It is my life now.

62

Easier Said Than Done!

"In conclusion, what the world needs is spiritual conviction, followed by spiritual experience. I would rather see a student of this Science prove its Principle than to have him repeat all the words of wisdom that have ever been uttered. It is far easier to teach the Truth than it is to practice It.

But the practice of Truth is personal to each, and in the long run no one can live our life for us. To each is given what he needs and the gifts of heaven come alike to all. How we shall use these gifts is all that matters. To hold one's thought steadfastly to the constructive, to that which endures, and to the Truth, may not be easy in a rapidly changing world, but to the one who makes this attempt much is guaranteed.

The essence of spiritual mind healing – and all of true religious philosophy – is an inner realization of the Presence of Perfection within and around about. It is the hope of heaven, the Voice of God proclaiming: 'I am that which thou art; thou art that which I am'" (Ernest Holmes, The Science of Mind).

As I read this last section of *The Science of Mind* called the *Final Conclusion*, I understand this is the simplicity of our teaching—to actively live the Principle and demonstrate it as our life. It is easier said than done and I believe it is a life-long endeavor.

I do not believe it is something that just happens. It is a practice, because as the world turns and changes, so we must meet new demands each day. The deeper we go into the practice of Truth, the more that reveals itself to us. The more that reveals itself, the deeper we go. We are a process, not a finished product. We are evolution, which is Infinite Intelligence unfolding and knowing itself through this experience called life as us.

We cannot just go around shouting, *God is all there is* or that *everyone is healed* when, although this might be true in theory, it is not a proven fact. Living it is the key to transformation. Living it when it has not demonstrated is the quest. We are *not to judge by appearances* and what better time to prove this than now. Ernest Holmes once wrote, "*The best time to work is when things look the worst.*"

Spirit is made to be lived here as us on earth. Otherwise, it will ever remain invisible and theoretical. I feel there is no greater school than earth right now. I am learning every day. What I mean by learning is that I am practicing to reveal my true nature amidst everything that I encounter every day. Spiritual Growth doesn't stop. Evolution is an ongoing process of unfoldment to the greater us.

Why do we learn through challenges? Hmm...that is a good question. I think it is the consciousness of the collective but I do not think it will always be so. We are asking ourselves to show up in greater ways and challenges are currently the way we learn. Sometimes we learn great lessons and move on and sometimes we repeat the same challenge over and over.

I believe that when we can get beyond saying *God is all there is* into truly living as God, no matter what, we will be practicing the Science of Mind and Spirit.

Keep in mind that the Science of Mind is not a religion that we are all supposed to convert to and live. It is a life Principle that states we must accept our oneness with the Divine and each other and live it. It's that simple and that difficult at the same time.

- When will we be able to look at others and see God instead of faults?

- When will we be able to live our authentic selves, no matter what anyone says?

- When will we choose love all the time?

- When will we take our expectations off of others and expect only the best from ourselves?

No matter what, we must stick to the Truth. Can we know the Truth when everything is pointing in the opposite direction? Can we live from this place no matter what? This is spiritual conviction - living spiritually, believing in the unseen, not judging according to appearances. If we can do so, we will know that we have not just said it, we have definitely done it.

Affirmation:

It is easy to see beyond every appearance to Truth.

63

Praise Everything!

19th & 20th Century mystic, Emma Curtis Hopkins, wrote, "*If I were to be asked directly as to the quickest way for a Scientist to get his healing power going, I would probably say 'Praise, everything and everyone in your mind, and speak these praises aloud.'*"

You might ask, how can I praise those things that annoy me? How can I praise my illness or my good friend's passing? This is not what Emma Curtis is talking about. She is not telling us to praise the events of life. She is telling us to praise God or Source at all times. She is telling us to praise our lives, our health, our abundance. She is telling us to praise our enemies by looking beyond what they are doing to who they truly are. I liken this to the story of the little child who made a mess. Her teacher scolded her, saying, "*You are a mess!*" The child retorted, "*I may have made a mess, but I AM NOT A MESS!*"

We are not a mess even when our lives feel disorderly. Praising everything shifts our attention to the Good we are experiencing instead of focusing on what is out of sorts. Have you ever been out to eat with someone who complains about every little thing but overlooks the good things around them and on their plate? Emma writes further about praising and complaining: "*Complaining and whining are only exhibitions of great desert spots in your character. You must fill up deserts with rain and fertilizer. So, you must transform your moments of complaining by praise and descriptions of the Good in the Universe. ...If things in your past have made you feel sad and hard, you must say the good they have done you makes you thankful. Give great thanks."*

Wow! This all seems like a steep order, but the act of praising and blessing does work to bring our mind and our lives to a greater sense of peace and faith. I love the Navajo tradition of "The Blessing" as proposed in Gregg Braden's book, *Secrets of the Lost Mode of Prayer*. It calls us to practice the ritual of blessing the victim, blessing the perpetrator, and blessing the witness. I recently did this exercise in regards to an issue of betrayal that has plagued me for a long time. I can say that it works. It is healing. The way of the blessing that the Navajo culture speaks of is the same as Emma's challenge to praise everything. It shifts our frame of mind and allows us to draw wisdom from difficult events in our lives and heal deeply.

I recently had a little experience that needed praising and blessing. This week we took our car in to have the shocks and back tires replaced. I left the repair shop with a smile on my face. I was grateful to have a repair person I could trust. The next day when I drove down to the beach to do my morning run, I opened the trunk of my car to find two old, dirty tires sitting on top of my grocery bags, sweatshirts, and my fanny pack. I was triggered. I literally lost it. I saw red. I started complaining loudly to my husband and casting thoughts of anger toward the car repair shop. All my trust and faith in the car repair shop went out with the dirty tires. I finally quieted down enough to say, "*I'm just going to go on my run and find out why this triggered me so much.*" I walked off briskly, literally using my hands to shake off the negativity I was feeling.

As I walked, thought, and treated for about a half hour (yes, it took me that long to calm down), I finally was filled with peace. I discovered it was all about my feelings of being disrespected. My trigger wasn't about the car repair shop. How did I know that this wasn't some big mistake? Everything is conspiring for my highest good, right? It either is or it isn't and I believe it always is.

I started my ho`oponopono (a form of blessing from the Hawaiian tradition) and there was my answer. I would call the car place to find out what happened, but then I had another idea. A quiet voice within me just said two words, "tire planter." I would make a tire planter out of those tires. I'd never heard of a tire planter before, but I was sure that was what I would do. I googled it to find a jolly British woman's YouTube video on how to make a tire planter.

Later, I spoke to the car place to find out that it was all a mistake and they had even charged me for the disposal of the tires. *"Bring them back or get a refund if you want to dispose of them yourself."* All I said was, *"I'll take the refund. I already took care of it."* Soon, I will have two new planters and I will have added to the blessing of our planet by not putting those tires in the landfill.

So, what's my point with this little moment of annoyance? Because of my calming treatments and my blessings, my mind got quiet enough to receive Divine inspiration. Emma Curtis wrote, *"We must woo and woo the Majesty and Responsive Beneficence ever facing us. Our wooing will be astonishingly rewarded."*

I invite us to praise everyone and everything, ever looking for the good in every experience. Please don't confuse this with masking our feelings. No, no, we must respect our feelings and look beneath them for their cause and praise that too. Be gentle and forgiving towards ourselves for everything. We are a work in progress, constantly revealing the greater self in every part of our eternal journey.

Who owns my mind? I often ask myself that following times like the one I described to you. I own my mind, even though sometimes I forget this. I am in charge of those thoughts that go marching through my head. When I remember who and what I am, who everyone is - the Divine, Love, God - all else will follow.

During these challenging times when there is so much we could fear or complain about, I have decided to choose faith and love. I am diligently working with myself to trust that everything is unfolding for my highest good, that people are here to help, that life is good, and that everyone is doing the best they can. I choose love above all else to move me through all the experiences I am having, from the death of people close to me to a small, irritating experience that can be part of my day.

I will follow the heart of this great healer, Emma Curtis, and *"Give glad, joyous praises every night, before going to sleep, to the Most High Good, that the Holy Spirit fills my thoughts with ardor, and fires my affairs to splendid achievements."*

Affirmation:
I praise everything. I give thanks.

64

Mother is a Feeling—A Message for Everyday

I write this on Mother's Day, but it is a principle I can live daily. As I think about everyone who has ever mothered anything or anyone, I realize that "mother" is a feeling. Yes, it is a person, but it is more than that. If mother were just a person, it would be contained and finite, and it is not. It is free and expanding. If mother is just an archetype, then we created that with our ideas of mother, handed down through the ages. That would make mother an opinion. It is more than that. If mother is just a body that gave birth to us, then mother would be relegated to this physical plane. Mother is an eternal Principle. Mother is a feeling.

There is a passage in Matthew 12:47 and 48 where Jesus is told that his mother and brothers want to talk to him. He answers, saying, *"Who is my mother and who are my brethren?"* He explained to his followers that in Truth each becomes the mother, father and brethren of all. Ernest Holmes goes on to say, *"God is the Androgynous Principle, the Father and Mother of all."* Our earthly parents symbolize this heavenly parentage. Jesus knew that love must become universal before it can reach its maturity. Hence, he said that all who live in harmony with the Truth are brothers, mothers, and fathers in it. Jesus knew that Mother was a feeling; an idea that connects us all when we realize that we are one.

I believe that Mother is a feeling. As a feeling, we all get to experience it whether we've had biological children or not.

If I understand that mother is a feeling, then I can celebrate mother today whether my mother is here on earth or has transitioned. If mother is a feeling, then we can celebrate the idea of mother even if we didn't have the best relationship with our own mothers.

Thinking of mother as a feeling allows me to open up to the nurturing of this word that we've created to explain the deep need each of us has to be cared for, accepted, trusted, and to trust. At one time, we lived in the womb in this nurturing atmosphere and then were birthed to survive in the world with or without motherly love. We've been clamoring to get back to that feeling of being nurtured and nourished and trusting. I think we spend our whole life with this in mind and that it colors everything we do. Some of us act out in the most negative ways, not even knowing that this is what we are yearning for.

Well, it is time now to know that we are nurtured. We are nourished. We can trust. There is an Infinite nurturer within each of us. It is our genius. It is our caretaker. It is the deep well of Spirit that never leaves us. It is always mothering us. If we reach out to Nature, she will show us the way. Nature is the teacher of motherhood. We can feel her within and without. If we just studied the story of trees and how they nurture each other, we would be transformed.

Mother is a feeling. Please do not forget it. Let us share the feeling of mother with everyone. Let it guide your path. I celebrate the feeling of mother today and all the people who have assisted in my experience of that feeling. I celebrate the Divine Principle of Mother.

Affirmation:
I embrace the Divine Mother within me.

65

The Power to Create Yourself

"On the day you were born, you were given the power to create yourself" (Bangambiki Habyarimana, Rwandan author).

Rev. Dr. Peggy Price shared this quote with us yesterday at CSL Kaua`i in honor of our Sunday message: "It's Your Birthday!"

I love this quote because it is succinct and speaks to me clearly in the middle of this pandemic we are all experiencing. On the day we were born, yes, we were given the power to create ourselves. What greater gift could we have?

We are definitely using this gift in every moment whether we are conscious of it or not. We do not have to be conscious of it to use it. It is a gift and reveals itself to us through the life we experience. When we consciously use it, we are so much more powerful in creating the lives we wish to experience. How many of us live by happenstance? Founder of Religious Science, Ernest Holmes, once wrote, *"Trained thought is more powerful than untrained thought."* It might be time to train ourselves to think from a higher place.

Over the last few years, I have become more and more interested in the experiments and findings of Quantum Science and Quantum Mechanics. Take this for example: *"The observer effect in quantum mechanics indicates that the quantum wavefunction collapses when an observation is made by an observer."* My husband and I sat and stared at a vase of flowers on our table and took in the idea that it was just waves of energy, collapsing into form as we observed it. I took a deep breath and thought about how significant this was.

This is a powerful concept for me regarding our reaction as a global community to the COVID-19 virus. We are all experiencing it in different ways; some of us more impactfully than others. However, if we've been given the power to create ourselves, we have the opportunity to experience COVID-19 any way we choose. We might not be able to change the physical facts for the world, but we can change our response to what is, and therefore, collapse those waves into new possibilities.

Are we afraid? Are we looking at it through the eyes of fear? Is it stopping us from expressing our lives fully? Or, are we resilient and are we reinventing ourselves in spite of it all? Can we imagine that it might not be here as soon as next week or are we thinking things are getting worse and new strains are coming? Are we a slave to COVID-19 or are we moving forward with our lives into greater and greater expressions of ourselves? I choose to focus on the new waves of creativity sweeping the globe.

Let's go back to the lyrics of an old song from the sixties sung by Janis Joplin, "*Freedom's just another word for nothing left to lose...*" Are we free or are we in a state of fear about losing something? When we fear losing this earthly life, our businesses, our families and friends, or anything in this earthly form, we are not free. And please, don't translate what I'm saying to "we do not care what happens to us or our loved ones." Of course, we care and have feelings about everything. Of course, we are compassionate and want to assist where we can whenever someone is suffering.

However, true freedom is complete and total surrender to the truths of eternity. Freedom is knowing that our journey doesn't end here; that we travel on an eternal road of expansion. Freedom is living each day as if it were our last and living it fully no matter what is going on in the world of conditions. Freedom is a commitment to responsibly using the gift of creating ourselves. For me, this responsibility would be to lovingly observe the waves of possibility that are presenting themselves and envisioning something new, expansive, and meaningful for ourselves and our world. If we've been given this gift of creation, and I believe we have, then it is our responsibility to use it with honor, love, respect, and an imagination filled with possibilities of good for all.

Affirmation:
I have the power to re-create my life.

66

Me and My Shadow

I heard the following story in a documentary called Discovering the Future.

> Once upon a time there was a man who went out to take a ride in his fancy sports car. He decided to ride these beautiful, windy roads through the country. He was having a great time, the wind in his hair, enjoying the fresh air. Suddenly, in the opposite direction, came another convertible, careening out of control. He swerved to miss the car, and as the woman in the other car whizzed by him, she screamed at him, "Pig!" The man was appalled, thinking how dare she call him a pig. She was the one out of control. Suddenly, he came around the corner and slammed right into a pig.

Now if this man had been driving through the back roads of Kaua`i, he would have had a totally different experience, because "pig" would have taken on a totally different meaning. Drivers have the possibility of hitting an actual pig here on Kaua`i. So it goes, our perceptions and beliefs are the lenses through which we see life.

Ernest Holmes, mystic, teacher and author, wrote, "*It is a beautiful and true thought to realize that every man stands in the shadow of a mighty Mind, a pure Intelligence, and a Divine Givingness.*" What we see in our objective experience is the shadow we cast as we stand in front of a Mighty Mind that is unlimited. We can limit our view of a life that is unlimited.

What does it mean to live in the shadows of our true self?

Last week, I reread Plato's *Allegory of the Cave*. If you are not familiar with it, simply stated, it is about a group of people chained in a cave, unable to move their bodies or heads and only able to look forward onto a wall. There is a fire behind them so they only see their own shadows and the shadow pictures displayed on the wall by puppeteers behind them. This is their reality. It is only when one of them is set free to explore the outer world and gets a glimpse of life in the light that he is expanded into the Infinite possibilities of something different. When he exits the cave, at first, he cannot even see because it is so bright. After experiencing the outside, he comes back to tell his fellow cave people about it. They laugh at him, telling him it's not true and that he is basically delusional. They cannot budge from the reality of their life in the cave.

I couldn't help getting excited about the idea that the limitations that I sometimes feel are only the training that I have received, the perceptions of the earth's collective consciousness, and my own walls of thought. Ernest Holmes writes about this: *"So every day we are living from this Unity (with God, Freedom, Law), and are projecting the experiences from it upon the screen of our objective lives. We have done this so long in ignorance that we appear to be bound by the outlines of the forms which our ignorance has projected."*

The shadows (our objective world) are so real that they have become our reality. I liken this to when I wanted to become an actor. I got another job, thinking that until I made it as an actor, this would keep me safe and fed. This made sense to me because my belief was that I couldn't make it as an actor. It might have been the logical way at the time, but the problem was my plan B became so real and secure that it became my plan A. My projection was real but I didn't realize that it was coming from my limited belief.

Now I understand and do my best to live from the greater knowing. When I decided to become a full-time minister, I understood and believed that this reality was supported by the Power of the Universe moving through me. My belief in this Power has expanded over years of study and practice. And this belief continues to support me as I sit here on the island of Kaua'i running a full-time, successful Spiritual Center. I know I am not finished so I continue to believe that I am expanding all the time. If I want a bigger life, I must change my consciousness. I must break my barriers of perception, my beliefs, and all that I thought was once true.

Ernest Holmes wrote, *"We can sit in the shade or move into the sunshine. Sitting in the shadow, we may not really believe that there is any sunshine. But, the sun would be there all the time; and all the time we are in bondage, the real freedom exists. It is there but we must awake to it. The Law of Mind as quickly creates one form as another for us and we must allow the patterns of our thought to become molded from the highest sense of Reality we possess."*

How many things do we believe that might or might not be true? We might wonder how we can know what truth is. It is that which edifies. It is that which expands us. It is that which moves us onto the high road of life, expressing our highest selves. It is us consciously evolving, following joy and passion, and by doing so, helping the whole world along. The world is calling for us to move out of the shadow of our limitations and create from a greater consciousness. I believe our very evolution depends on it.

Affirmation:
I let go of limitations and create from my greater consciousness.

67

Getting to Know Me

"You are not just in the Universe; the Universe lives in you." I heard these words by mystic, philosopher, and author, Jean Huston, as I embarked on her course this morning, *Using Your Quantum Powers.* We know enough now, scientifically speaking, that gives us the understanding that we are entangled in a Unified Field that responds to our perceptions and observations. The philosophy that states that we create our reality, moves past fiction, and into the realm of unlimited possibilities and pure potentiality.

I can see how the reality I live is different than that of my family, for example. I don't play by the same rules. One is not bad or good; it is just different.

When we meet someone new, we usually ask a series of questions. I am being inspired to get to know myself in a new way every day. I ask, who am I? I am a human playing in a 3-D world, but I am also a Quantum being playing in an infinite field. What does this mean and how does this impact my life? If I want to change my financial situation for example, I can plan and balance my check book, start a savings account, invest in stocks, and other possibilities.

However, there is another field of creation that influences all of those possibilities. It is my belief, my ability to imagine, my faith in myself and my intelligence, my ability to attract others that can guide me, etc. All of this comes from the invisible. Just staring at the world of form and manipulating it physically based on past statistics and future predictions without my intuition and use of imagination and will is limited. My Quantum self has no limits. It is working with unformed substance and realizes that it is my beliefs that set the limit to what I can create.

Firstly, I need to step out of my old beliefs. I love the term "mental hygiene." Jean Houston uses it as another way of saying, clean out your mental closet. We all have beliefs and it is a good thing to acknowledge those beliefs. You'll know what you believe by looking at your life and your experiences. We attract that to which we are equal. If we want an upgrade in our life, we have to be willing to replace those beliefs with new ones.

Ernest Holmes, author and Founder of Religious Science, once wrote that the first thing we needed to get when getting anything is "understanding." What do we believe about the Laws of the Universe? Do we understand them and trust them? Are we willing to experiment with the Law of Cause and Effect, the Law of Mental Equivalents, or the Law of Correspondence? Can we experiment with the idea of "so above, so below," or "so within, so without?" Beginning where we are, we must come to understand ourselves working in relation to these laws.

Can we accept that there is more than we see in front of us? Can we admit that perhaps we do not know anything and open up to know something new? Can we get to know our true selves by being willing to meet ourselves in meditation and then take our discoveries out into the world and prove them? Can we accept that we might just be bigger and greater and more expansive than we ever imagined?

In the early 20th and late 19th centuries, something happened that was quite amazing. At a time when we relied on spiritual authority outside of ourselves to tell us what was right for us, the old ancient thoughts that were once known on earth began to be reborn through what we call the Transcendental Movement and the New Thought Movement. Not everyone felt this way but there was a definite surge of longing to know more. We realized we could heal our bodies. We explored the idea that perhaps we were our own authority and didn't need an outside force to tell us what to believe. We began to realize that God or the Universe was within us and we needed no mediator to process the truths of the Universe.

At the same time, science was making new discoveries. There was a growing investigation into invisible theories about our minds, our brains, and our very cells. Magic was being born on earth, after a long, dreadful time of believing we were finite and predetermined beings that were moved around like chess pieces by some greater Power.

Now, at this time on earth, these discoveries of inner power are accelerating. It is time to really get to know ourselves, our true selves. The whole universe lies within us with all the answers to everything we would ever need to know, even if we were to never pick up another book. I happen to love learning, exploring, reading, and listening to new people and philosophies. However, in the true Reality with a capital R, if I was stranded somewhere with no books, internet, or another soul, I know that everything is within me and knows the answer to everything.

So, let me introduce you to myself. I am consciousness. I am just beginning to learn what that means. I am capable of manifesting the life I desire in whatever way I choose. There are no limits. I can co-create in the Quantum field by expanding my consciousness and recognizing my true identity.

Why am I here to do that? I believe it is because, by doing so, I am serving the world and my co-inhabitants and aiding in conscious evolution. I am here to create a more loving and infinite planet by recognizing my own loving, infinite, cosmic nature. I am here to release limitations and become unbounded. I am here to bridge this life to the next and the next and to realize that the only time is the present. I am here to live in time and space as a 5th dimensional being so I can play in time and space instead of letting it dictate to me what I am.

You are all the things that I am and have available to you all the wisdom and power of the Universe. It is written in your cells, implanted in your DNA. As Carl Sagan once wrote, *"The nitrogen in our DNA, the calcium in our teeth, the iron in our blood, the carbon in our apple pies were made in the interiors of collapsing stars. The cosmos is within us. We are made of star-stuff. We are a way for the Universe to know itself."*

Affirmation:
I am made of star-stuff.

68

Safe Travels!

On April 5, 2021, the Safe Travels program was put into effect here on the island of Kaua`i. Travelers can come here without quarantine, provided they have proof of a valid negative COVID-19 test. Some of us are elated and some of us not so much. I am in the elated category because I know how important tourism is to our island. Many people have been impoverished through the last year of this pandemic due to lack of work and the shutting down of many businesses. Of course, there have been many blessings, too. The number of COVID-19 cases on our island are below 300.

So, now what? Safe Travels signifies that we should feel safe. Do we? Those who are vaccinated say that they feel safe and the tourists are free to come. There are those who are not vaccinated that feel safe also. There are some who do not feel safe at all, in either case.

My questions are: what is this feeling of safety, when will we feel it, and will we be able to sustain it? As I understand it, the COVID-19 vaccine doesn't guarantee that we will not get COVID, but makes it less likely that we will die from it. Do we still feel safe? I am not advocating vaccines and I am not advocating not getting vaccinated. I am just asking a question. When will we feel safe? I'm sure we have all known people who have left their home in the morning, only to never come home that night due to an accident or some catastrophe. Did they feel safe when they left the house in the morning? Every day we are confronted with many reasons beyond COVID-19 that could challenge our feelings of safety. Do we feel safe in this uncertain world?

I guess it depends on what we define as safety. If safety is a sense of feeling free from physical harm, then I would say it would be difficult to ever feel safe. However, if we define safety as knowing that whatever lies before us, there is something within us that always keeps us safe, not necessarily physically, but safe from fear, confusion, and all limitations. We feel safe because we know that we walk with and as a Power that is greater than any obstacle in our path. Our feelings of safety come from faith and trust that we will know what to do in any situation.

I believe that we are coming to a time in our evolution when it is more and more necessary to trust our Higher Power. I believe that a new life is being born and that we are understanding that we are more than these mortal bodies. We are coming to understand that the Universe lives within us, with all its powers for life and creation. I believe we are being called to rise above our conditions in the world to a higher consciousness that puts us at the helm of our destiny as a species.

I have been told it is a fact that we are on the verge of the sixth mass extinction as a planet. All roads point to it. We cannot solve our problems anymore, nor have we ever, from the same consciousness that created them. We must start living in cooperation, oneness, and Love. We must put down our weapons of separation and begin to understand and accept each other right where we are. Let us not use COVID-19 or any political view to turn ourselves against each other. Feelings of safety are individual and we can respect each other as individuals.

We live in this world based on our perceptions. The mystics have always known this and the new discoveries in science now concur. It is done unto us as we believe. We all have different views on everything, but it doesn't mean that we cannot get along. We do not have to be right in order to be safe. As long as we do not live destructively toward others, we can succeed. We can overcome our separation. We can live in oneness. To me, this is the promise of a safety that is indestructible and eternal.

Affirmation:

I live in safety because I live in oneness.

69

Intuition: the Tool for Challenging Times

Things do not seem to be working very well right now as we wait to see what the "new normal" will be. I have had more conversations with people lately who seem scared and uncertain about their future. People often come up to me and ask me if I hug. I am sixty-eight years old and I never ever imagined that I would be asked that question for the reasons it is asked today. Why would I be afraid to hug you? The reason, under the surface, is because you think that I might think that you will make me sick.

Families have been kept apart even at the most crucial time of transition for this reason. Yesterday, while I was meeting with a friend outside at the hospital, a young girl told me of her grandmother who was ready to transition. The girl was afraid that she wouldn't be able to be with her grandmother because only one person was allowed in the hospital room at a time. Do you remember the day when families stood around their dying family members to witness this important moment? Something is not right.

I understand that we are in the middle of a pandemic and that people are dying. What I don't understand is how the fear of dying could hold back our deep necessity as human beings to touch, hold, and to be together. Something is not right. When someone asks me if I have been vaccinated before I am allowed to come to their house party, I say something is not right. What I do with my body is my personal freedom. I am a logical person. I am an intelligent person. You are an intelligent person. You are a logical person. I invite us to make decisions based on the deep well of our intuition and not on an ever-changing reality, a shifting sand of opinion. I could give many examples of the illogical nature of this reality but I'd like to switch gears and talk about how I deal with all of these challenges.

I live a spirituality that is deeply ingrained in my consciousness after over twenty years of practice and education. This spirituality is scientific in that I know it is true for me because I can prove it. It tells me that I live in a Field of unlimited possibilities and that everything is potential in that Field. It is done unto me as I believe and what I focus on with feeling and passion, manifests. I am in charge of my reality and my reality presents itself to me through my beliefs and perceptions. I could be in the same exact situation as you and perceive it totally differently, creating an entirely different experience. You might be having a nightmarish time, while I am calm and at peace, or vice versa.

So, in regards to the world right now, I know that I get to experience it through my own beliefs and perceptions. I get to turn tragedy into wisdom and anger into a call for love. I am free because I am a spontaneous expression of something far greater than what is in the world. In fact, everything in the world comes from this far greater Source, as we are all entangled and expressing in a multitude of ways. I trust that the Universe is a caring Universe. I trust that when I look at someone, I am looking at a healthy person, unless something tells me otherwise; in which case, I am still looking at a healthy person on the spiritual level.

What does it mean when I say "spiritual?" It means that I trust the invisible essence of things and understand that everything begins in the invisible. There is an Energy from which we all come that has never been touched by experience and is ever-changing, recreating Itself, and is always whole.

How do I maneuver through these challenging times? Firstly, I understand that love is the strongest energy that there is. I do my best to stay in a consciousness of love. When I find myself sinking into the rabbit hole of fear, I pull myself out by centering and refocusing my energy. I know I am always at choice to do this. I also have others that can help me when I can't refocus. I have like-minded people who will throw me a rope of Truth when needed. I remember that the doings of the world right now are created by consciousness. What a thought has done, a thought can undo. I trust this theory because I have proven it and know that it works. I also live my life trusting in the Power of the Universe as Wholeness. I understand that the Universe moves as Life, not death. Even in death, there is Life. We live in a living, breathing Universe and It lives within me and within you.

My prayer (which is a movement of energy) for this time on earth is that more and more people will catch the recognition of their own Spiritual superpowers - intuition, choice, decision, faith, and, most of all, Love. As Ernest Holmes says, "*Love is a Cosmic Force whose sweep is irresistible.*"

Nothing can overcome Love, not COVID-19, or fear, or doubt, or lack. Love heals all. If I pray for anything, it is that we will be kind to each other and see the highest and best in all of creation. Oneness and unity will prevail. We will gain wisdom from the current challenge; a wisdom that will catapult us into a consciousness upgrade that will transform this planet and heal it from separation. It all begins with me and with you.

Affirmation:
I live my superpowers now.

70

It's a New Day

It's the night before Easter and the ending of Passover. I am here with a lot of thoughts of what Easter and Passover mean to me as a New Thought Minister and an evolving Spiritual Journeyer. I am not a Christian, but I do love and honor the Master Jesus. I believe he was the embodiment of Christ Consciousness. I also believe that he specifically wanted us to follow his example. What was this example? From what I read and intuit, it is to love one another. It is also to come to know that we are God and that the Power and Presence of God works through us.

I believe that we are capable of all that Jesus accomplished, but only as we come to truly know ourselves, our true powerful selves. As we embrace the Power in us, we can do anything. If Jesus died for anything, it was for the Truth for which he stood. It was threatening to the political and religious powers at that time.

So, when I celebrate Easter, I celebrate the birth of my True Self, the rising of my consciousness, the giving up of the old and no longer useful - fear, doubt, lack, anger, etc. When I am using the word Truth, I am speaking of unconditional love. I know that if we practice this kind of love, the troubles of the world will melt away.

I also know that it is my perception of what is that changes me and my circumstances. I can look at everything as a tragedy or as a miracle. I can come to accept that life changes and this means that there will be goodbyes and hellos as I move through life here on earth. I understand that nothing is permanent and that everything is meant for our evolution. I am up for whatever is placed before me because I have the spiritual tools: innate qualities of resilience, wisdom, intuition, and so much more. This tool chest constantly expands as I meet the challenges and opportunities of life. It's all here for us.

I heard a talk this morning by Brother Ishmael (African mystic, founder/spiritual director of the Etherean Mission in Accra, Ghana). He said something that struck me. He said that we must accept that this is a "caring Universe." He mentioned all the reasons this was true, from a mother caring for her child, even doing tasks like changing diapers with a smile, to the cat that greets us pressing up against us and welcoming us home. It is a caring Universe. He repeated this idea of a caring Universe so many times in so many ways that I got it. Try repeating "*It's a caring Universe...*" and bring to mind the many reasons why. You will be changed.

When I think this way, everything is new. I am comforted because I know that the Universe has my back, no matter what. I am resurrected to a higher state of consciousness. I am liberated from the slavery of negative thinking that holds me in place in limitation and morbidity.

I've lost a lot of people I love over the last couple of years. It is unbelievable in some ways how many have gone out of this world. However, I can choose how I think about this. If it is a caring Universe, then I have to see this as a loving change. I have to know that I am comforted and can find comfort in spite of my loss. I have to know that my loved ones are safe and are right here.

There is a quote by Nona Brooks, the 19th Century healer and mystic, that goes like this, "*It is by the process of resurrection that we rise out of the contemplation of that which is hidden, the mysteries as we have called these, into the full light where everything is made clear. There is nothing hidden that shall not be revealed to the one who sees the unity of life. We are rising into recognition of the glory process, when we stand before a blade of grass and see that even this is wonderful."*

On this Easter Sunday and on this last day of Passover, my prayer is that the clarity required to move through this challenging time on earth will be embraced by more and more of us. My prayer is that the fear that seems to shroud the joy of life will fall away into the abyss and that the Light will shine. I know that I am responsible for this clarity and to be this Light. We all are. If I truly see the Unity of Life, I will see that every stone matters, every word I speak matters, every blade of grass is wonderful. It will be a new day for no other reason than because I am new.

Affirmation:
It is a caring Universe. I reflect on the many reasons why this is true.

71

Are You Root Bound?

Have you ever experienced working with a potted plant that is root bound? If a plant is root bound, the roots completely take up the pot, circling round and round and creating a mass of roots. The plant cannot grow. In fact, eventually it will die because it has nowhere to get its nutrition from. It's literally strangling itself. To save the plant, we must replant it in a larger pot.

It's the same way with us. We can get root bound. I do this when I am telling the same story over and over. I am telling a story that doesn't serve me. I think I am making myself feel better by telling it, but really, I am just creating a circle of roots in my subconscious that are growing round and round and producing nothing but the same story. That story manifests in my life again and again. *Wherever I go, there I am!*

Well, in order to free a root bound plant, what do you do? You have to replant it. But first, you have to rip those roots and sometimes cut them. When you are doing this, it is important to remember that plants are tough.

In order to free my root bound life, I have to have the courage to rip my mental roots apart. I have to have the faith to try. I have to know that I am tough enough to take it. I have to look at my beliefs that keep those mental roots constricted and be fearless enough to change them.

When you free a root bound plant, you take the plant out of the pot, spread the roots apart, and put them in new soil. The same works with us. We need new soil, new ideas to nurture our beliefs. We need to water our new beliefs with faith and then take action.

A good gardener will tell you that they've rarely lost a plant by freeing its roots. In fact, the plant has flourished and grown in new soil.

I know that sometimes we think it is easier to stay in the same pot and to not make a change in our life. It's uncomfortable. Motivational Coach, Bob Proctor, would call it "*walking through a terror barrier.*"

When I feel change coming, I admit that I start to feel uncomfortable. I know that the pot I've created is my life needing expansion. It needs a bigger, more spacious container. I am the only one who can make this happen. It takes faith that I'll be okay. It takes a leap into the unknown.

We must start right where we are, not jumping too far ahead. We must ask if our consciousness is ready for the jump into a bigger pot. Consciousness always comes first. I might not be ready for an open field. I might not be ready to walk on water. However, from my slightly bigger pot of consciousness, my life will begin to grow upward. It's guaranteed because life is always expanding and spiraling upward. If you look at your own life, you will see this is true. It's only when we stay stuck or root bound that we live a life of stagnation. We are meant to grow, to flourish, and to expand.

I invite you to begin today. Take those mental roots out into the open and take a good look. Don't be afraid. You are tough and ready for the change because of the Power that lies within you— the biggest Pot of all.

Affirmation:
My consciousness is expanding and I am living an expanded life.

72

Becoming the Thing

Life is eternal and self-existent and creates by becoming the thing it makes. We are life and this is the way we create our life experience. We become it in consciousness.

So, you might ask how do I become something? Let's say I want a new car or more money? How do I become a car? We have to go deeper than this. These are merely effects. The act of becoming is an act of feeling. We live in a quantum universe that is made up of waves and particles. Particles are our experiences that have taken form, but we always have the opportunity to be more wave than particle. One way we can practice this is by focusing on our inner world. When we move into a state of pure energy, a field of unlimited potential, we can create the new. It is a mental act of the Spirit.

How do we get there? My way is through first telling myself that I can. Then, I free myself from the world of conditions through meditation. I sit until I have changed my state of being. If I am feeling lack, I sit in meditation until I feel the abundance of the Universe moving through me. Gratitude is a sure way to create a mental embodiment ready to receive as it puts us in our heart space. When we have gratitude, we are opening our field to receiving more for which to be grateful.

This might sound airy-fairy to some of us, but to tell you the truth, it is scientific. It can be proven by each of us if we care to put it into practice. We must not be afraid to really look at our lives and our so-called troubles and accept our part in it all. We must start where we are, and then realize that we can move into a greater state of consciousness, big enough for all we say we want in our lives. We must be single-minded about it. It will take changing the thoughts we were thinking that were holding our troubles in place. We must observe and change our thoughts.

There is no room for doubt. If we doubt, we must work on our doubt. We must believe before we see the outcome. This is where the feeling comes into the formula. What does it feel like to have health, to have wealth, to be creative every day, to be in loving relationships? If you can feel the outcome and then step out and act as if it were true, no matter your outward conditions, you are on your way to "becoming the thing."

Right now, I am working on something very specific. There is no sign of it in my life in the world of form. However, I can feel what it would be like to experience it. As soon as I move into this feeling place, pictures of it begin to flash into my mind. Sometimes they do not make sense, but I just let them come.

I remember when we first began to create CSL Kaua`i, people would ask where our physical site was, and we would point to our hearts. That was the truth, and eventually it moved into form in the way of people, places, and things. We started with what we had, which was our consciousness. We had a great feeling of love and passion behind it. We walked out as if it were already true and did our part.

We all have consciousness and we all have access to the Field of Unlimited Potentiality, but we cannot get there with the baggage of our past, or even our current troubles and woes and longings. We must be willing to start new and to continue to let go and surrender. Ernest Holmes once wrote, "*We all stand in the shadow of a Mighty Mind.*" We are the ones that cast the shadow. It is us. Step out of the way, and let the light come through. It's here, right where we are. Take a breath and let go, and believe in all that is possible for the mind that believes that it is God, the Divine, and Unlimited.

Affirmation:

I take a breath, let go, and I know that my good is here now.

73

Challenges Turn to Wisdom

The year 2019 was probably one of the most challenging years we have had in our Center, and at the same time, one of the most rewarding times. We've traveled through multiple deaths, financial setbacks, and human conflict within our community and in the greater global world. However, from these experiences has come great wisdom. Yes, we have literally turned our challenges into wisdom. We all have this same capacity. Out of challenges come wisdom when we choose to look deeply enough into our reactions to those challenges and take responsibility for our part in the experience.

Dr. Joe Dispenza, neuroscientist, author, and educator, has spoken on the idea of getting locked into the emotional reaction we experience from a traumatic event. Every time we relive that trauma, we relive the emotion. This creates a cycle. Our bodies are not meant to be in a constant stress mode and eventually these repetitive emotional experiences will take their toll on our health and well-being. Is this what we want, or are we willing to make the necessary corrections to our thinking so as to live a more fulfilling and joyful life? Please do not confuse this with not feeling your feelings. Beyond those feelings is healing- when we claim it.

I've had a new awakening these last few months when the spiral of tragedy surrounding and directly involving me seemed to accelerate. I was bombarded daily with a new challenge causing me to sometimes lose my spiritual footing. Even with my daily meditations and numerous daily Spiritual Mind Treatments, it wasn't enough to armor myself for each new challenge. I talked myself into thinking I didn't have enough time to take even more time for myself when it was needed.

What was causing the enormous stress I was feeling? It was because I was allowing my energy to bleed into actually thinking I could stop the challenges from coming, compounded by feeling that I had to fix it all.

I cannot stop others from dying or stop others from grieving. I cannot make people choose differently. I cannot be everything to everyone. I cannot create abundance from a consciousness of lack. I cannot stop people from talking about me negatively. These are all effects and behind them is some belief. As Sadasivanathaswami from the Kaua`i Hindu Monastery said, as he pulled a weed from his garden, "*We must pull the weed in our mind from the root so it will not grow back.*"

It is the same in the Science of Mind teaching. Behind every effect is a root mental cause, and until we let it go, we will keep repeating the same effect.

The experiences and the things in our lives are reflections of our consciousness. If we have a consciousness of trouble lurking around every corner, trouble will definitely show up. This idea showed up for me when I retold a story I'd already worked hard to release. As soon as I did, the old emotions came up, and *voilà*; shortly after, the story showed up again in another form.

This is a simple philosophy that can be difficult to practice. As Ernest Holmes wrote, "*We make a riddle out of simplicity.*"

I choose to make it simple all the way around. I choose to garner the wisdom of these last few months and use it to move forward. I choose to look at what I want to experience and become those experiences in consciousness. I choose to shift my consciousness by releasing beliefs that no longer serve me. I choose to take as much time as I need for myself to be successful in this practice. If I've learned anything from these past few months, it is that self-care is mandatory.

By taking my necessary steps in shifting my consciousness through self-care, my experiences will shift. It's scientific. It can be proven. I've already proven it both negatively and positively.

I decide to walk on the positive side of life with purpose and vision for the future. Effects are mere shadows of my mind. When my mind is stayed on the Truth of Love, and when I think and walk out from that place, only then will new plants of experience bloom.

Affirmation:
I garner the Wisdom from my past and move into a new state of being.

74

Where Are You Looking?

This week I had an experience of hosting a meditation at our Center. It was amazing. One of our Spiritual Coaches guided us deep within. My heart saddened a bit afterwards when I contemplated on the fact that only five people attended. I was confused. People said they wanted healing. People ask for meditation. Where were they?

Today, I stop myself and I reconsider my thoughts of that evening. I see that I was looking in the wrong place. I was putting my faith in numbers. I was deciding success was based upon who showed up. This is a perfect example of how our ego can trap us. Yes, of course, we want numbers because we want to reach as many people as possible. However, looking to the outside for our success will only create longing for more and more approval. Our answers and strength must come from within.

I do what I do because this is the way Spirit is expressing Itself through me. I choose to give my energy and light to the world. I am not responsible for how it is received. I have no idea what is occurring behind what I see in front of my eyes. Instead, I know that every time I put my energy out into the atmosphere, it is received everywhere—seen and unseen, near and far. And so, I continue to do what I am called to do. I do not decrease, but I increase. God/Source is always expanding.

I challenge myself not to look to the outside for my approval or success. I look deep within to the roots of my being and know I am always a success. I look for more ways to increase my experience of giving.

Whatever we are doing in our lives, I invite us to know that it is enough if it is coming from our true Heart Center. Some people will ask me, "*Why am I here?*" I say it is enough that you are right here being who you are. It is perfect.

Affirmation:

I look to the inside for my approval, and I feel the love of the Universe moving through me.

75

Tongs, Centipedes, and Free Will

I have had many experiences with centipedes since moving to the island of Kaua`i. Once I was bitten by a centipede that was hidden in the folds of my laundry in my outdoor washing machine. I was not expecting that. I hadn't learned the ways of rural island living.

Slowly, I've come to learn more about the ways of living on an island. Now, for the most part, centipedes present themselves to me in clear daylight so that I can remove them from my presence. Just this morning, that occurred. I am grateful for danger presenting itself to me. I consider this a gift from the Spirit that proclaims my safety at all times.

So, what's the metaphor here? Well, we are constantly reminded of danger presenting itself in the way of negative thinking. The emotional charge is our warning. It arises so we can heal and transform our thinking and not ignore those feelings. Just like the centipede, in plain view, these thoughts and emotions that don't serve us are warnings of what will come if we do not take care of them. If we live unconsciously, they are still lurking in the washing machines of our subconscious, just churning over and over without a rinse cycle.

It's all about love and forgiveness. It's all about taking the responsibility for the beliefs that lead to the thinking that destroys our peace of mind. We have the opportunity to either take the tongs of choice and remove the belief, or we can ignore it and then wonder why our lives do not change, why we cannot demonstrate our heart's desire, and why we cannot heal.

The Universe is always in our corner. It is set up for us to be successful. Things are in plain view, even if they are in our subconscious. People ask, "*What if I don't know what those things are that are holding me back?*" We do not have to know. All we have to do is look at our lives and we will see what we are believing and thinking. Being willing to really see our lives as they are, and then to use our inner power to make the changes necessary for a better experience, is what free will is all about. We get to replace those beliefs with new empowering ones. We are not victims; we are powerful creators of our destiny.

We do not need to fear bringing our subconscious out into the daylight. There is a Power stronger than any outside condition. It is within us and is our ally. It is more powerful than a pair of tongs when confronting a centipede. It is the Power that moves through all of creation. It is the Power for change, the Creative Process, Cause and Effect, Love and Law.

Affirmation:
I look fearlessly at my life and know I can change any condition by changing from within.

76

Do We Create Our Diseases?

I have been accused on occasion of telling people they created their illness. In fact, this is a prevalent criticism of those who investigate the Science of Mind and other New Thought philosophies. What do we truly teach about this subject? Do we profess that we create our diseases? The answer for me is both yes and no.

No, we do not decide one day that we are going to develop cancer, or for me recently, that I would develop a severe tooth infection and sinusitis. That is not the way It (God) works at all. There was a time in religious belief systems when people were blamed for their illnesses and told that sinning was at the root of all disease and a punishment from God. In the Science of Mind, we do not believe in this sort of God. God is only Love and we are only Love.

The Law of Mind and Spirit creates from Itself and we live in a state of Grace when we are conscious of this Love. When we become ill or suffer from disease, God (Love) is here within us every step of the way. For me, disease is only here to bring us back to our Truth, or Divine Identity. It is an effect of the collective consciousness of the world and is felt by many of us as real and constantly available to be experienced. The necessity of disease is a belief very much ingrained in the subconscious.

There is a Principle of the Science of Mind that states, "*We believe the ultimate goal of life is to be a complete freedom of all discord of every nature and that this freedom is to be attained by all."* If we look at this one passage deeply, we will see that it doesn't state that we will have no discord, but that we will be free of it. What does this mean? I will bring it to my own example with my dental journey this week. Although I suffered from the physical aspects of this experience, I did not suffer mentally. Instead, there was peace and an opportunity to go deeper within. I was willing to acknowledge the dis-ease began in the mental field and I was willing to clear and drain away the old beliefs. I was willing to embrace a new, loving thought about myself. That, for me, is freedom from discord.

So, the above is my "no" answer about the personal creation of disease. The "yes" part might be a little harder to digest because it means taking responsibility, not for the physical disease, but for the discord in our mental atmosphere that comes in the form of self-condemnation, unforgiveness, and an inability to embrace the good for ourselves. These are good reasons to continue to torture ourselves with disease, and not just those that affect our physical bodies. What of financial disease?

It all comes back to self-love and the willingness to penetrate the depths of our beliefs and to heal them. Does this always bring healing in the body? This all depends on the person. Healing is not always physical healing, but it is always emotional and mental healing. Quantum Science attests that negative emotions locked in the body live on and will eventually manifest as some sort of disease unless they are healed and released.

So, you can see, that this answer as to whether we create our diseases is profound and takes deep introspection, accompanied by gentleness and lots of self-love. It is not about blaming ourselves or continuing to struggle with "trying to heal." It is about getting so up close and personal with the Divine Presence within us that the healing journey begins, and the layers of consciousness peel back deeply, again and again. Life is eternal and this is an eternal journey of our evolution.

And another thing to clarify this: Science of Mind philosophy believes in all types of healing, including medicine and doctors and physical treatments. There is a beautiful passage in The Science of Mind on page 219 that says, *"Since our spiritual understanding is not sufficient to enable us to mentally set bones, we call a surgeon; since we cannot walk on water, we take a boat. We can only go as far as our spiritual knowledge takes us. ...Do not let anyone discourage or belittle your efforts by asking, 'Why don't you walk on water? Jesus did.' ...If we had the understanding which Jesus had, we would be able to walk on the water."*

In conclusion, for now, I believe dis-ease is human made and not God ordained. I also believe as soon as we accept our Divinity and Perfection, we will not travel this route, and instead move into a higher order of being.

In the meantime, if we experience any type of illness, instead of giving ourselves condemnation, give ourselves lots of love and kindness. As we look within to our Healer for our answers, if we choose, we can work in tandem with the medical world. We will always know the correct path for ourselves, when we truly seek to know it.

Affirmation:
I love myself as I am. I am healed and perfect.

77

Things are Gonna Get Easier

It's my birthday and I am beginning my new year. My husband, Rev. Patrick, is responsible for teaching me to appreciate my birthday, to honor it, and to create my new year on this day. What does this look like? Well, the questions I ask myself are, "*What do I want to experience this year? How do I want to live? What do I want to receive and what do I want to give? What is my intention for this year?*" I then proceed to spend my birthday living the answers to these questions.

This goes beyond goals and resolutions. It is about gratitude and feeling. It's about making decisions and setting the Law of my Being into motion in a specific direction. I use Spiritual Mind Treatment to do this. It means that I have the opportunity to decide how I will live this year no matter what occurs in my life. I recognize everything is occurring through me and for me. There are no loop holes in this philosophy for me. I take full responsibility for my life and my experiences.

The last few weeks have been a bit difficult and challenging. We lost our beloved cat, and right after that, I developed a serious tooth infection. I began a dental journey which takes me into my new year. I feel the healing. I've attracted the right dentist and I am surrounded by love. It is not what happens to you; it is how you choose to experience it. We are at choice. As I stated in one of my previous blogs, our

Declaration of Principles in the Science of Mind states that we will be free from all discord. I choose that freedom now.

I woke up this morning with a song on my lips. It was a song from the 1970s by the Five Stairsteps. It was called *O-o-h Child*. Perhaps some of you from my generation remember it. It says, "*Things are gonna get easier,*" and then, later in the song, the lyric is, "*right now.*"

What if things were to get easier for all of us right now? What if we were to turn our challenges into wisdom? What if we were to let go of the strangle-hold we might have on "how" we think life should go, and instead, allow life to flow through us for our highest good? What if we accepted our good right now? What if we realized that we totally deserved our good?

On this, my birthday, March 12, 2021, I claim this for everyone! Life is getting easier right now. I claim that everything is falling into perfect place and love is prevailing. I claim more and more good is available for all of us. I claim whatever we have lost this year, whether it is someone close to us, our possessions, or our jobs, that that loss is creating an opening to allow us to heal, to prosper, to start anew, and to expand. We are garnering the wisdom from everything and we are moving forward to an even greater life.

Happy Birthday to me and Happy New Year to all of us.

Affirmation:
Things are gonna get easier...right now!

78

Let Not Your Heart Be Troubled

I have an outlook on all that has occurred and is still occurring in this world of conditions. I believe in the evolution of our soul as individuals and as a planet. I believe that beyond the worldly conditions, something great is unfolding. I believe the more we turn inward for our answers, for our strength, for our love, we will receive the guidance we seek. I believe each of our lives is unfolding perfectly and none of us are ever lost, even if we pass from this earth. I believe we are held in the arms of Grace and Love will win. I believe everything is the unfoldment of the Great Presence that moves all of us to know ourselves deeply and to love each other without limit.

Forgiveness is the key to a more loving life; forgiveness of ourselves and of others. The parents who brought us here, whether they were the best parents in the world or the worst, were the vehicles that got us here and not the destination of what we can be and experience.

As we learn to appreciate the wisdom gathered from our past and let go of the emotional tie to our misery, we move forward into a greater expression of ourselves. If we are suffering right now, we can be healed. As we turn to Life, Life turns to us.

I believe in myself. I believe in you. I believe in us because we are an individualization of the One Source of all Life. We might feel like we've been left here alone, but I believe we've been left here to discover ourselves. When we do discover ourselves, we will realize that we have never been alone. The Life Force that birthed us is the very fiber of our cells, our mind, our soul.

Let us not faint in discouragement. Let us use our discouragements to find out what it is we need to know more deeply. In every pain there is a treasure. If we think of the pearl hidden in the grit of the sandy shell, we might understand we are that pearl and sometimes we have to reveal it through the grit of life. We are spectacular. We are Divine Intelligence. We are Love. We are eternal. We are our own answer and the answer to every question in front of us.

Affirmation:
I am a treasure, a beautiful pearl.

79

Remember the Stars

"We do not will things to be done, things are brought into being, not by will but by the power of the self-assertive truth."

I love this quote by Ernest Holmes. Willpower is exhausting and will not get us far in making anything happen. A self-assertive Truth has its own power. It is the strength of a strong intention sent out into the Field of Unlimited Potential with feeling. It gathers its own strength and attracts everything that is in like vibration. I liken it to a snowball rushing down the hill, gathering speed and more and more snow at the same time.

My favorite time of day is the early morning before the sun rises. On one particular morning, in the midst of all the turmoil during the week of January 6, 2021, I was in great need of some kind of peaceful feeling. I was caught up in the news and waiting for outcomes that would bring peace. I forgot for a moment that one can never find peace from the outside. Peace, like all the attributes of Divinity, is an inside job.

I looked out the window from our bed. There seemed to be more stars in the sky than on previous mornings. It moved me to walk outside. I stood looking up at the clear, velvet sky as my little cat came to weave his body in and out of my legs and beg to be petted. I appeased his persistence, but I kept looking up in the sky. I was deeply struck by how immense and infinite it was. I was struck by the idea of how undisturbed it was by anything that was happening in the world. I contemplated the idea that the stars remain constant amidst the daylight. When the sun rises, those stars won't go away. They will simply fade to the greater light – the Sun. However, they will still be there shining no matter what occurs during the day.

I felt more peaceful in that moment and more aware that, beyond everything we see, there is always more. I felt more connected to the Power greater than the world of conditions. I was ready for my day. Now, if I fall into the trap of getting caught in the world of conditions, I have a mantra: "*Remember the stars.*"

How do I take this mantra and apply it to a Truth, so self-assertive that it moves with its power into manifestation? It seems quite simple. My intention is to live my life using more of the Infinite Power within me to bring Good forth amidst the chaos. The reminder that there is a constant behind everything temporal allows me to feel secure, safe, and willing to experiment. It informs me that behind the transient world is the Changeless on which I can rely.

Ernest Holmes wrote, "*There is one Life aback of everything that lives. There is one Energy back of all that is energized. This Energy is in everything. There is One Spirit back of all expression.*"

Evil is the misuse of the greatest Power, the Power of choice moving through Law into form. Anytime we seek to control through hatred and anger, or anytime we focus hatred toward ourselves, we are misusing this Great Power. We have forgotten who we truly are—LOVE.

It is important during this challenging time in our evolution to learn how to control our inner world. I believe self-exploration, self-nurturing, and lots of faith in the Principle of Life will move us through successfully.

"*Remember the stars.*" They burn bright and constant within each of us, no matter what. We are built for these times.

Affirmation:
Today, I remember the stars!

80

It's the Thought that Counts

When I was a little girl growing up on Long Island, I didn't have any money of my own. I didn't receive an allowance nor did I have any way of making money. However, every year before Christmas, my grandma would give me $5 to go out and buy presents. That was a lot of money to an eight-year-old. I remember walking down to the local dime store to spend my fortune. I'd enter the store and look for special gifts for my mom, my dad, my aunt, and my grandma. I remember finding a punch bowl with cups and a ladle for my mom and dad. It cost about $2. I would buy my aunt a bottle of what I thought was the fanciest bubble bath. I remember giving my grandma some special smelling powder. And, of course, there were cards to go with the gifts—all covered by my $5.

I was very proud of my gifts and couldn't wait for everyone to open them on Christmas morning. It was a wonderful feeling to see their faces and to experience their appreciation. I don't know if they ever used those gifts or really liked them, but I know they appreciated that I wanted to give them something.

Giving was a huge part of Christmas for me. I will always be grateful for my grandma teaching me about the giving of gifts. I learned that no matter how small or big the gift is, it is the thought that counts.

For me, it is important to remember this today when a lot of pressure is put on us to buy presents at Christmas time. We are encouraged by advertisers to spend more than we have. We are taught the bigger the present, the better it is. I could fall into the trap of giving beyond my ability in the world of form, but instead, I remember that it is always the thought that counts the most.

I remember one Christmas several years ago when we had so little money that all I could do was write my kids Christmas notes telling them how much I appreciated them. I told them the truth and admitted that this was the best I could do right now. It didn't feel good at the time, because I wanted to give more. However, now as I look back on it, I see I was doing my best with what I had. It was the thought of wanting to give that mattered.

I believe that the gift of giving is really for us. When we give, it awakens the power of gratitude within us for others. No matter what we give, even if it is a note or a phone call long overdue, we should hold our heads high and give with all our love.

Love is the gift and many of us need a lot of love right now. The pandemic of 2020 has separated many of us but we never have to be separated if we continue to give the gift of ourselves. No matter how it is received, always remember, the giving is about you, and how big your heart is open to that giving.

This year I have a little more to spend on gifts but I can still feel it is not enough. Then I remember that little girl that went shopping at the dime store and she reminded me that it is always the thought that counts and my love is always more than enough.

Affirmation:
Giving my love is always more than enough.

81

Emergent Evolution is Real

When the Universe makes a demand upon itself, it meets that demand. It is called emergent evolution. Ernest Holmes wrote, *"It is the kind of evolution that takes place in the necessity of the condition."* In other words, there is a solution for everything.

I am a firm believer in emergent evolution. It is the necessity to evolve that resides within each of us. I tune into this power anytime I am up against a challenge in my life. For example, if I am hit with an unexpected financial challenge such as a sudden need for repairs to my car, I affirm to myself that this demand wouldn't be here right now unless I had the supply to take care of it. I affirm there is something within me that meets the demand I am facing. The Universe is conspiring in my favor. I have practiced this truth over and over until it is accepted at my subconscious level.

We live in a Universe that is backed by Consciousness. Some call it a mental universe. Please don't confuse this with trying hard to think our way through life. Yes, our thoughts send signals out into the Field of unlimited possibility, but it is our feeling that brings the experience back to us. It is a feeling Universe.

Our thoughts come from our beliefs. All of our beliefs are held in our subconscious mind. We have the power to reprogram our subconscious. Through practice, I have reprogrammed my subconscious to believe that the Universe meets the demands of my life whether they come in the form of financial challenges or health challenges. The quantum science experts might tell me that I have rewired my brain to fire differently, and therefore, I am living my life from a new reality. I attract the outward experiences that match my new reality.

I invite you to work with your subconscious programming, knowing that you have the conscious power to do so. Meditation, affirmations, and Spiritual Mind Treatment are my methods. It takes practice, but it is an exciting adventure.

I believe during this time on earth, it is mandatory to know that we do have the power within us to respond to life as we choose. We don't have to be swayed by everything that comes our way from the media and other outside forces and conditions. We have the power to earnestly inquire within and get answers. We have the power to respond from a higher order of thinking. We have the power to change our beliefs when necessary.

The Universe is demanding a change in consciousness and it has to meet that demand through each and every one of us. It is emergent evolution. Are you ready?

Affirmation:
I have the power to respond to life as I choose, no matter the outside condition.

82

Bliss Gone Viral

December has begun and I have witnessed more people in the Holiday Spirit than ever before. Immediately after Halloween, lights started going up everywhere. What my husband calls cross-decorating was prevalent throughout our neighborhood. Thanksgiving was on the horizon and Christmas lights with pumpkins and Thanksgiving décor appeared.

Why the demand for the holidays to be here and be here now? Humanity has an innate desire to be happy, to have joy. It is our birthright and definitely implanted in our DNA. Dr. Ernest Holmes once wrote, *"The Original Life is Infinite. It is good. It is filled with peace. It is of the essence of purity. It is the ultimate of intelligence. It is power. It is Law. It is Life. It is in us. In that inner sanctuary of our own nature, hidden perhaps from objective gaze, 'nestles the seed of perfection.'"*

We know it. We feel it. We can trust it. I feel a true movement toward this knowing. It might be showing up in the desire to get our decorations up. It might be showing up as we feel the desire to tidy up our homes or to give more smiles to others. It might be showing up every time we find ourselves saying enough to the doom and gloom of the news. Bliss has arrived and it is going viral.

But, what of the suffering, the illnesses, and the businesses that are closing one after another? On our island of Kaua`i, the return of the 14-day quarantine for tourists stands to hinder our economy once again. These are the facts, but they are not the Truth. The Divine Presence is greater than all of this and the Divine Presence is manifested in and as each of us. It's time to renew our minds and to think of new ways of being and creating. Because the original Life is ultimate intelligence, and that Life is our Life now, there is nothing that we cannot achieve.

Joseph Campbell urges us on in his famous quote, "*Follow your bliss and the Universe will open doors where there were only walls.*" We might see plenty of walls in the world of form, and if we keep reinforcing them with our fears of lack and illness, plenty more will continue to be built.

I believe I must continue to follow my bliss in an even greater way and bring that bliss into manifestation. I believe that when I follow my bliss, I am powerful. I have witnessed the Universe opening doors where there were only walls.

There will always be something else to block us if we put more trust in the conditions of the world than in our inner perfection. It is time to individually get in touch with our inner guidance and allow it to speak to us and direct our path. It is time to bloom.

Let us go viral with bliss. The Universe is on our side. I invite us to trust the Invisible Infinite Power and get to work.

Affirmation:
I go viral with my bliss now!

83

Living on Easy Street?

Judge Thomas Troward, mystic and 20th century author, claimed that the reason for our existence is to be happy. If we truly think about what this means, we would logically agree that if everyone was truly happy, the world would be a heavenly place. Everyone would be fulfilling their heart's desire. I believe happiness is contagious.

Ernest Holmes wrote, *"We see the abundance in the Universe. We cannot count the grains of sand on a single beach. The earth contains untold riches, and the very air is vibrant with power. Why then, is man weak, poor and afraid? The Science of Mind deals with these questions."* He then answers his own question with, *"The Divine Plan is one of freedom; bondage is not God ordained. Freedom is the birthright of every living soul. All instinctively feel this."*

Do you feel free or do you feel like you are in bondage? Is your feeling of freedom or bondage conditioned by your experiences, or is it a feeling that comes from within, no matter what is occurring in your conditional world?

We are free, whether or not we appear to be. Some would argue with this. They might say that not everyone is free. They might argue that some might not be born under the right circumstances to enjoy freedom.

This is not the freedom Ernest Holmes is talking about. He is talking about the freedom to choose what we shall think and what we shall believe. Thoughts are things, and as we choose to think a certain way regardless of our circumstances, our lives change. Sometimes we think we cannot change our thoughts. We must delve deeper. It is our beliefs that create our thoughts. It is our beliefs that need changing. Everything is belief.

What is easy street? *"Easy street is a situation in which things are easy and comfortable for you."* I claim easy street for all of us today. I believe that we can have a life of ease and grace and I do not believe that it comes from having everything go our way. It comes from being able to ride the ups and downs of life with an attitude of gratitude and a deep faith. It is in realizing that we are the storm and the tumultuous river. We have everything within us to meet every challenge.

We are the creators of our destiny and everything is calling us back to ourselves. To look at the dark times as well as the light times with a knowing that everything is happening through us and for us is the sign of a Master. I want to be a Master of my life.

I do not seek to change things but to change my consciousness around those things. When I do, then the experience shifts. Even if I cannot see the sun on the other side of the storm, I can still know it is there. I know that everything is temporary and good is here right now. The more I trust this and have faith in it, the more my outer conditions begin to shift.

We might live in a world that learns through suffering. However, suffering is not our destiny. When we are done with suffering, we will begin to learn in a whole new way. Easy Street is a life that is lived in the flow while at the same time realizing that we are co-creating that flow.

How do we get to Easy Street? Here are few ways:

- Gratitude – If I can find reasons to be grateful instead of getting swallowed up in any experience, I shift.

- Releasing the past – I'm here now. Whatever I did in the past has passed. The present moment is where I can make changes.

- Trust – There is always more that's going on than meets my eye. Can I trust what's happening behind the scenes, that perhaps there is a bigger plan for me?

- Taking Action – If I say I want something, then I must begin to take steps toward it. I do my part and ask the Universe to do its part.

- Surrender – sometimes I have to surrender my way. This is not a cop out. It just means I have to stop manipulating others and forcing things. Am I trying to change someone else? If so, I must stop it and change myself in relation to the situation. I must surrender my small finite self to a higher version of myself.

- Respect for myself and others – Do I have enough respect for myself to speak my truth when needed and also listen to others with an open heart?

- Clarity – If I am clearly intending and clearly walking the path of love, then it is easier to speak my truth without worrying what others are thinking about me.

- Affirmative Prayer – Prayer works, and when I truly use it and trust the Law of my being to make my prayer so, my life gets easier. My prayer is always for the highest and best outcome. I get out of the way of how it happens. I fill my prayer with calmness, ease, and grace.

Suffering is caused by resisting what is and not living powerfully in the present moment. Evolution is about overcoming the past, living in the present, and dreaming about the future.

Easy street is for all of us strong enough to know who we truly are. Easy street is for those of us who trust the Laws of the Universe, and in turn, learn how to work them. Easy street is for those of us who give up thinking small, and instead, open up to live bigger, more loving lives.

Easy Street isn't about "sleeping 'til noon." It is about the choice to stay awake, knowing it is the best day ever and we wouldn't want to miss any of it.

Affirmation:
I live powerfully in the flow of life and my life is easy and graceful.

84

Let's Harmonize Together

"The Nature of First Cause is that it is harmonious. If there were an element of inharmony, discord or decay anywhere in Its Nature, It would destroy Itself" (Ernest Holmes).

What is First Cause but the Unified Field of Intelligence, the One Energy and Source. It is constantly pouring Itself into the Soul of the Universe through each of us. We, in our true essence, are harmonious, whole, and perfect.

As we look out into our world, it might not seem harmonious. For instance, at this time in history, we see our very own country appearing quite divided and inharmonious. However, this is only an experience in the conditional world. The more we can recognize harmony and wholeness within our own lives, the more we will see it manifest in the world.

We have come to a time in our evolution where we are being called to know and love ourselves so completely that we only see with the eyes of harmony and wholeness. We are being called to practice the Law of Love in the world. No one can be left out of our hearts. We might not condone what someone does, but we do not have to lock them out of our hearts. We can step out of judgment and release whatever it is in our own hearts that projects that judgment outward.

I work with the practice of Ho`oponopono which directs me inward to release anything in myself that is creating lack of harmony in any experience. As I go through my own process of forgiveness, I am uplifting the One Mind in which we all live. I always close my Ho`oponopono practice with Spiritual Mind Treatment. You can read more about the powerful practice of Ho'oponopono in the book *Zero Limits* by Joe Vitale.

We are beautiful waves of Intelligence and Love that make up the One Unified Field. It is a breathing, living, eternal Field of Intelligence filled with information. Because we have choice, we can do what we may with our use of It. However, we can never separate ourselves from It or from Its innate Nature of Wholeness and Harmony. We can only think that we are separate and this is why we suffer.

As a wave of energy in this Unified Field, our nature is like It - creative. I invite us to begin to use this power of creativity to bring more harmony into our experiences. I invite us to actually put it into action. We are each so important.

Affirmation:
I accept my place in a Field of Wholeness and Harmony.

85

We Can Be Kind

"We can be kind. We can take care of each other. We can remember that deep down inside we all need the same thing" (David Friedman).

I love the lyrics of the song *We Can Be Kind*. The notion of kindness is so simple, and yet, seems to be difficult for so many of us. I am convinced that everything is unfolding just as it should and it is up to us to bring peace to the world. We cannot expect to have peace if we are not peaceful within our own lives. We cannot expect to have a more loving world if we are not loving. We must heighten our practice of the simple act of kindness. We are being called to be the change.

Dr. Ernest Holmes wrote, *"One's mind should swing from inspiration to action, from contemplation to accomplishment, from prayer to performance."*

So, let us find reasons to be inspired and to be kind and then let us take that into action. Let us contemplate kindness and then live that contemplation fully. Let us pray for our world and then go forth and act as if it is already so.

INSPIRATION • ACTION • CONTEMPLATION •
ACCOMPLISHMENT • PRAYER • PERFORMANCE

It is time to think before we act. Think before we speak. *"Is it true? Is it kind? Is it necessary? Will it make the situation better?"* Asking ourselves these questions before we move into action or conversation will lead us into a more kind and more peaceful world.

I am grateful for this time of heightened awareness. Everything is coming up to be healed. It's up to each of us. We are the healers and the healed.

Affirmation:
I am inspired to be kind and to take that kindness into action.

86

More Than Meets the Eye

I know there is always more than meets the eye. What does this mean? Only that what we see, we see from where we are in consciousness. There is always more than meets the eye because consciousness is always changing, expanding, and growing. As Wayne Dyer once wrote, *"When we change the way we look at things; the things we look at change."*

So, let's take a little trip into ourselves and possibly embrace the idea that there might be more than meets the eye.

I am more than the molecules, atoms, and cells that are my body. I am the very consciousness that holds them together, projecting their form as me. I am ever-changing. I am more than a body. I am in a body. I am in charge of my emotions, and as my emotions change, my body keeps time with the music they make. I choose gratitude, compassion, and love.

I am more than my checkbook as I do my best to make the numbers match what the bank says I have. I am more than meets the eyes looking at these numbers. I am the energy beyond and behind these figures. I am the substance that is in constant activity, unlimited, and taking form exactly as I believe. Can I conceive? Can I believe? Can I accept there is more here than what I see? I choose to live in an unlimited Universe and to give gratitude and appreciation for what I have, always knowing there is more.

I am more than my job. I am more than what I do every day.

I am the energy that repels and attracts experiences. Every moment, I give myself permission or deny myself permission to be my best. I am not my promotion or demotion. I am unlimited source and creativity unbound no matter how others label me. I choose to give my all and know I am always met with all that I am.

I am more than anything I call an accomplishment. I am the soul who is on a journey back to its highest self. Everything I experience is that journey, not the label I put on the experience. There is no such thing as success or failure. I choose to look at everything as an opportunity to grow and expand.

I am more than my relationships. People are reflections of me. I am the builder or the destroyer of relationships. I am either love or an absence of love. I am in exact right relationship to everyone and everything.

Because I know that I am more than meets the eye, I know this is true for each and every person. Therefore, I release judgment and only see with the eyes of love. No matter how someone else is behaving, I know there is more than meets the eye. God's perfection is always expressing itself. I am at choice to see it and embrace it in everyone. The more I can accept God in everyone, the more I can accept God in myself as a perfect unfoldment of right action.

Affirmation:

There is always more than meets the eye. I choose to embrace this holy practice and to see beyond appearances.

87

Increase Your Spiritual Bandwidth

Bandwidth is a term used to describe how much information can be transmitted over a connection. To increase my bandwidth means I can transmit more information at the same time. Bandwidth is the size of the transmitter which determines our upload and download speed.

It is the perfect metaphor for increasing our capacity to express the Infinite Spirit. I am the transmitter for Spirit. As Ernest Holmes wrote, *"We cannot contract the Infinite, but we can expand the finite."* That would be our own bandwidth, our conscious connection in Spirit, and our capacity to expand it.

The difference between download and upload speeds can be explained in the following way. Download speed refers to the rate that digital data is transferred from the internet to your computer while upload speed is the rate that online data is transferred from your computer to the internet.

Increasing my spiritual bandwidth allows me to download Infinite Intelligence at a greater level of embodiment and also expands my capacity to upload or give. The Law of Circulation is increased as I increase my ability to embody the concept of Infinite Spirit. There is a play between uploading and downloading speeds. Sometimes one or the other needs more of my attention. I will know when and what is needed.

However, I have to play with the Universe. I have to open

up. Ralph Waldo Emerson wrote, *"Every man is an inlet and may become an outlet for all there is in God."* We are already inlets. We cannot stop the Universe from pouring through us, but we can stop ourselves from recognizing it. We are always at choice. How we identify ourselves in relationship to the Universe is our path to becoming an outlet. Being an outlet means our ability to let the Source Energy flow through us and out. Can we believe Rumi, who once wrote, *"We are the ocean in a drop."* Can we believe that the whole of the Universe exists within us?

When we are experiencing speed issues on our computers, we are sometimes instructed to connect directly to our router with a wire instead of using a wi-fi signal. Similarly, we need to make a direct mental connection with the Power within us instead of floundering in space and time wishing and hoping something in our lives will change. We do not need a mediator. We do not need someone else's power. And we do not need someone else to tell us we are okay or good enough. We need to make a direct connection. This we do by means of the gift of intuition.

Another instruction we are given to increase our internet speeds is to clear our temporary files, history, cookies, and cache. Deleting these files can increase the overall speed of our computer. In turn, this will increase our upload speed.

Similarly, how can we move with power and newness when we are carrying all our old files with us. Beliefs might need changing. We definitely need to let go of beliefs that do not serve our wellbeing. Our view of Reality and God might need renewing. Are we open to change?

You might be asking, *"How do I do that?"* It starts with a decision to say yes to believing there is an unlimited Universal Energy pouring through us, and to say yes to experiencing it at a deep, intimate level.

I was walking on the beach earlier this week right after sunrise. I looked at the expanse of a beach that was literally almost empty, just me and the ocean. It was beautiful, breathtaking. I thought to myself, how did I end up here? I was most definitely experiencing Heaven. I know it wasn't because I am fortunate. I am no more fortunate than anyone else. The Universe is impersonal and it doesn't play favorites. A voice within me said, "*You chose this.*"

Yes, I did choose. I chose to follow my heart and to always take my next step. It isn't always easy to choose the life we want. The choice I made almost a decade ago to live on Kaua`i came with the faith that the Universe would back my decision.

Ernest Holmes wrote, "*Here and now we are surrounded by, and immersed in, an Infinite Good. How much of this Infinite Good is ours? ALL OF IT! And how much of it may we have to use? AS MUCH OF IT AS WE CAN EMBODY.*"

He screams out that we can have ALL OF IT. He screams out that we can use AS MUCH OF IT AS WE CAN EMBODY.

If we want to embody more of the Infinite Good of the Universe, we have some work to do. It is daily work. It comes down to turning within and increasing our dependency on Spirit, surrendering to its activity, relying on it. It takes looking out with eyes focused on what we want to see. It takes surrounding ourselves with positivity. Not just positivity in lip service, but true positivity; the kind that only seeks to see the good in everything; the kind that is willing to praise everything. Even if there is only a pinhole of light, we have to find it and expand it.

Gratitude is the best way I know to increase our bandwidth.

Starting right where we are, we can be grateful for everything. We can be grateful to be alive during these strange and challenging times.

This question is asked in *The Abundance Book* by John Randolph Price. "*Have I expressed a deep sense of gratitude to the Spirit within before my good comes forth in visible manifestation? Is my heart overflowing with thankfulness and joy the majority of my waking hours?*"

How great is your gratitude? How great is your God? The answer to those questions is in how big your bandwidth is.

As we increase our own bandwidth, in turn, the magnetic field of the earth is increased. John Randolph Price also wrote, "*The Good of the whole must begin with the Good of the individual. You help the world when you help yourself. Remember we are all waves in the same ocean, and one man's consciousness of wellbeing and abundance with its outer manifestation releases more light into the race-consciousness for the benefit of all.*"

Affirmation:
I increase my own bandwidth and the whole world benefits.

88

I Used to Think that Way Until I Didn't

I remember when my daddy used to sip his coffee in the morning and talk about the richness of life and how he appreciated every part of it. He savored the physical existence. I remember my mother telling me that before he passed away, he would watch the orange tree that he had planted outside his window, waiting for the oranges to ripen. He made his transition before they ripened. This story has always made me feel sad, until I knew better. I changed my consciousness about it.

I developed a similar way of thinking to that of my dad's. I love this life and I love my coffee in the morning. I love the physical aspects of watching a sunrise and drinking in the beauty of a tree swaying in the wind. I've said things like "*This could be my last sunset.*" I used to think that way, but something has changed.

One day, I simply realized that I could never miss a sunrise or even the sip of hot coffee. When I leave this physical existence, I will merely become those things. In fact, I already am everything, and that is why I can feel anything at all. Nothing is outside of me. It is called Oneness. We could never miss the sensations of beauty we feel in this life because we already are the beauty.

I don't know what it was that made me believe this way. As I said, I just began to think this way with no seeming effort on my part. Perhaps this is what happens when we dive deeply into the Spirit of things, when we take the time to live the Spiritual life.

I am always taking a class or reading a book to assist me in growing my consciousness. Today, I thought, can a teacher change us? Can he or she get us to begin thinking in a different way or change our lives for the better? The answer I came up with is *no*.

Teachers all stand at the door and knock. They point the way. Teachers teach from what they know and feel and have experienced. However, in the end it is up to each of us to take the journey. We are the ones that must make the change in consciousness.

I love to do Spiritual Mind Treatment for people when they ask me. However, I know that they are the ones doing the changing. The Law directs the course of their request, but they must get into the flow and open up to receive their answer.

No one can live our lives for us. I can't teach you to know that you become the sunset. My journey might inspire you but you must take the journey in your own way. What happens to each of us happens in our own soul.

Affirmation:
I take my own individual journey and always receive my own answers.

89

The Parable of the Oranges

I was out running one Sunday morning when I passed the most beautiful orange tree, overflowing with oranges. I had passed this tree before, but on this particular day, it looked more inviting. *"How juicy and sweet a fresh orange would taste,"* I thought.

I was running on a path that brought me back to the tree more than once. When I circled around again, I saw a man picking the oranges. Again, I thought, *"How great a fresh orange would taste. I'd love to ask for one."* I ignored my inner longing. It would be too embarrassing to talk to someone I didn't know.

When I circled around yet another time, I passed the same man who was now carrying a large brown bag filled to overflowing with the oranges he had picked. He looked at me and pointed to the oranges, gesturing for me to have some. Was he reading my mind? I took one from his bag. The man looked at me rather strangely and kept walking.

I continued my run. A few moments later, I passed the man one more time. Again, he gestured to the oranges in his bag, silently offering me another one. I took another orange. He looked at me and groaned out loud, seeming to say, *"You idiot! I'm offering you as many as you want!"* He shrugged and waddled on down the road, leaving me holding my two oranges and two questions.

First of all, why couldn't I ask for an orange? Secondly, when the man offered me as many oranges as I wanted, why did I only take two? I could use the excuse of being polite or not being able to carry them, but there is really only one answer to these questions. This orange story is a metaphor for my capacity to receive.

In that moment, I immediately turned my attention to the truth of who I am and opened my mind to the abundance I deserve. I opened up my mind wide to allow the abundance of the Universe to pour through me without limitation.

Ernest Holmes says: *"In Reality, we know God or Truth only as we ourselves embody God or Truth. AND SINCE IT IS IMPOSSIBLE TO EMBODY ANYTHING OUTSIDE OURSELVES, THIS KNOWLEDGE MUST BE AN INNER LIGHT."*

I didn't feel the expansion at first, but as I continued to spiritually work on this idea every day, my consciousness began expanding. I challenge all those who need this knowing to join me in doing this spiritual work for themselves.

The answer for me is self-love. Ernest Holmes writes, "...above all, I have a consciousness of love, a radiant feeling flowing through your consciousness at all times. Treat yourself until you have an inner sense of unity with all good. Love is at the center of man's being and the calm continuous pulsations of life are governed by love."

I still pass that orange tree every day, and I still wonder if I'll ever see the man again so I can take as many oranges I want. It hasn't happened yet so today, I said to myself... *"What are you waiting for...just go buy yourself a huge bag of oranges!"* And so I did!

Affirmation:

I open up and receive the abundance of the Universe now.

90

Fences

A while back when I had just become a Spiritual Practitioner, I was out running, contemplating a treatment I just wrote. The Treatment was about knowing that I am one with the Divine. As I started to run, I said, "*I bless this time to reveal this to me now, and to inspire me for my power talk that I am to give this morning.*"

I was about 10 minutes into my run when I noticed a fence, and then another, and then another. I noticed, metaphorically, how every yard, whether by brick, wood, or rock, was boxed in. I was awakened to the fact that it seems to be our nature as humans to separate.

The question came into my mind, "*What fences do you still have up, Rita, that are keeping you from totally embodying your oneness with Spirit?*" What am I trying to keep out and what am I trying to keep in?

There must still be fences of thought that separate me from embodying my Divine Nature. Thoughts of "being less than, or not being enough, or separation from others" came to mind. I spoke out loud, "*I choose to tear down these fences of separation now!*"

I continued to run, and every time I saw a fence, I metaphorically tore it down in my mind. It took quite a few swings with my metaphorical ax, but soon I was running immersed in the Allness, and there were no fences.

So, now what? I continued to do this all day. Every time I

saw something from which I separated myself, whether it was my boss, the person asking for money on the corner, or the biggest and most beautiful house in the neighborhood, I took down the fence.

Robert Green Ingersoll, lawyer, orator, and freethinker said, *"Surely there is grandeur in knowing that in the realm of thought, at least, you are without a chain; that you have the right to explore all heights and depth; that there are no walls nor fences, nor prohibited places, nor sacred corners in all the vast expanse of thought."*

As we know in the Science of Mind teaching, everything is created from the inside out. There is nothing created that isn't created first by thought. Our thoughts direct the Law.

Today, I challenge us to tear down any fences of thought that keep us from total immersion in our Divinity. Right now, we are God. We don't have to do anything or be anything more.

Affirmation:

All my fences fall away now. I am unlimited Life!

91

Divine Intuition

On Saturday, December 19, 2008, we dedicated the permanent labyrinth that we built at the California Rehabilitation Center at Norco, California. The events that led up to this blessed day began one night in a spiritual class when Dr. James Mellon claimed that a labyrinth would be built in the room where we were meeting. He spoke about the room being lit with candles and people walking the labyrinth. Immediately, I felt called to accomplish the task. A few days later, using masking tape, we outlined the shape of the classical 7-circuit labyrinth on the floor. Shortly after, we had our very first labyrinth walk at the NoHo Arts Center for New Thought. Although we did not know it, this event was one on a timeline that connected thousands of lives coming together.

Since that night my fellow practitioners and I traveled throughout Los Angeles, from cemeteries to hospitals to beaches, facilitating labyrinth walks with our community.

Then, in September of 2008, it was time to introduce the labyrinth to the inmates of the California Rehabilitation Center (CRC) at Norco where we my husband and I had been doing theater and empowerment workshops. Adding the labyrinth to our work created a profound change in the hearts and minds of the inmates. It was a testament to the power of the labyrinth as a tool for personal insight, inspiration, and transformation. It was also a testament to following our divine intuition. As Michael Beckwith, founder and spiritual director of Agape International Spiritual Center, said in one of his inspirational talks, "*The entire Universe is conspiring to release its energy through us.*"

Spirit is intuiting through each of us for the greater good. We all have claim to this intuition in our own unique way. We all have a gift to give; we only need to listen deeply and then act on it. The Universe makes the way possible even when we do not know how it will happen. The permanent labyrinth we built at CRC Norco is a demonstration of that.

The inmates expressed their desire to have a permanent labyrinth. Up to that point, once a month, we were carrying in a portable labyrinth to share with them. Although we did not know how it would occur, we said yes to the permanent labyrinth.

Before long, we were moved out of our regular meeting place at the prison. We were disgruntled at first, but finally gave in to the change and opened up to our new space. Lo and behold, there it was in the courtyard – a perfect spot to build our permanent labyrinth. In the reality I know, I believe that labyrinth found its own way to CRC Norco through the inmates' desire and our decision to make it so. Then, of course, we had to take action. With the help of the inmates, we designed and built it.

The story doesn't end here. When we conducted labyrinth walks, we always brought handmade angel cards with us. These cards are just little slips of paper cut into one-inch squares with inspirational words written on them such as "peace, joy, forgiveness, gratitude." They are called angel cards because they have a picture of an angel on them. They are meant to be picked up on the labyrinth and add focus and inspiration to the walk. The night before the dedication, I was writing cards and a word came to me that I found rather strange. It was the word "helper." I almost passed over the thought because I couldn't imagine how that word meant anything. I stopped analyzing it and I thought, "My intuition brought it to me so I better write it." So, I did, right next to that angel picture.

During the sharing time after our walk, a very young inmate raised his hand. He was very emotional. It was his first few weeks in prison. He missed his daughter and felt awful about having to leave her. The first card he picked up on the labyrinth was "helper." It was the translation of his daughter's name which meant "angel helper." This inmate received this card as the message that his daughter was with him.

I know we are all here to allow Spirit to intuit through us. We are here as part of a big picture called LIFE. All of us matter. We are each an integral part of the matrix of life. We must never underestimate the power of what Spirit can do through us. We are definitely conduits for the Universe. On that day so many years ago when I said yes to the labyrinth, I know I began a chain of events that changed lives even beyond my knowing.

Sometimes we have the opportunity to see the fruits of a decision, and sometimes we just have to trust that when we get the inspiration to do something and follow that inspiration, good is always transpiring in time and space.

Affirmation:

I am always listening and living by my own intuition.

92

My Decision Process

I'm about ready to make another big decision and I want to be clear. As I sit down to meditate, my mind starts to wander. Instead of listening, I am listing all the pros and cons of this decision. I am reflecting on the negatives and positives. How can I get clear when I am thinking instead of listening, and how can I get quiet enough to listen?

I settle in my chair. I get in touch with my breathing. My mind starts to wander again. I bring myself back again. As I finally settle into the quiet, something becomes very clear. Something just doesn't seem right. I've had this feeling before while making decisions and I've ignored it. What ensued was trouble within the experience.

The trouble I was feeling was something in the subjective field that might or might not happen. It was my doubts and fears. I was picking up on it. This is called being psychic about something. I read something in my own subjective field and I colored it with my own perception of it. If I were to go to a psychic and ask them to do a reading for me, they would read my subjective field and they would give me answers that were colored with their perception of the situation.

There is something else much more trustworthy. It is called intuition and I can rely on it in this decision and in every part of my life. As I sit quietly in my meditation and commune with the Spirit within, leaving the outside world of conditions, a clarity fills my mind. I know all the answers are within me because I think in and from the Mind of Infinite Intelligence. It is always clear and it knows it is not about the physical decision; it is about the life I want to live. Does this decision fit a life of peace and love? Is it leading me in the direction of serenity? Does it fill me with the knowingness of prosperity and abundance?

As we move down the road of life and its many decisions, it is important to reflect on who is making the decision. Decisions that pull us here and there with no understanding of the core of our True Nature are whims and hunches. Decisions that are clear come from our highest knowing. They are not so much about what we are doing, but what we are being.

Recently, someone I know was about to make a decision about her job. She had a tempting offer and she was confused as to whether she should take it or not. In fact, she hadn't even been looking for a new job. The job came to her. I asked her, *"Would taking this job lead you in the direction of your overall life goal or is it just a great opportunity that you think might never come again? Why are you thinking about taking it?"*

Sometimes, we think this is the only time, the only chance. However, that is not true. Opportunities never exhaust themselves. To the Soul who knows Itself, there is always another opportunity to grow and expand.

So, in summary, all my answers lie within. When I have a clear sight about the life I want to live and how I want to live it, my decisions are clear and come easily. I know that wherever I go and wherever I find myself, the Power and Light of the One Spirit is always with me, as me. Whatever the course I take, where all is possible, I leave the future and bring myself to the here and now. I know the answer because it feels peaceful and right.

Affirmation:
I trust my inner guidance, and my decisions are clear and come easily.

93

Are You Waiting for Perfection?

Last night we had the honor to be at a friend's birthday. It was so much fun. What I loved the best about it was her clarity on what she expected from her celebration. "*It's going to be a lot of fun,*" she declared at the ending of her opening speech. I loved watching that clarity unfold as we all took part in her manifestation. It was one of the best birthday celebrations I've ever witnessed.

It is not the first time on Kaua`i that I have watched parties unfold with such love. People give from deep within themselves—dancing, singing, poetry, and speeches from the heart. I am always in gratitude for living in a place where people share deeply from their core.

As I think about this, I am reminded that something doesn't have to be perfect before I share it. I used to be a perfectionist, holding back until I felt that what I had to give needed to be in operatic form - all my high notes in perfect pitch. I am reminded of my dad telling me once, "*An aria is not about one note.*" He would say this when I would be terrified all the way through a song, dreading the one note that might crack.

Life isn't about one note. It is about living. It is about putting ourselves out into the world from the deep place within, with all that we are. Our so-called flaws are not flaws. They are as much a part of our identity as every perfect thing we think we have done. I want to live a life unafraid and authentic.

I want to be a space where others can feel the same in my presence.

Truly sharing ourselves in deep authenticity from right where we are is freeing. I witnessed that at my friend's birthday party. Love permeated every sharing. In fact, as I think back on the evening, I am left with the big smile on my friend's face as she witnessed and felt her birthday wish come true. An evening of everyone having fun was her declaration at the beginning of the party, and that is what I remember.

Life isn't about one note sung perfectly or a perfect pirouette. If we waited for that, we would never live. Life is a symphony of individualized creative beings who express themselves from the deep well of love - right where they are, as they are. It's sheer perfection!

Affirmation:
I am always perfect.

94

What About Me?

I'm looking for balance today. I feel that I've gotten so involved in the happenings in the world that I have forgotten that I am important too. Without becoming an ostrich who puts her head in the sand, I'd like to get back to me. If I am holding back my own life because I am so invested in thinking about the state of the world and how I can fix it, I am definitely not free.

I realize most of my time is spent in my head, but what do I have but the power of my own mind? My mind acts upon the Law of the Universe and brings me back exactly what I put into it. I have not been spending my mind time well, and I will change it now.

This week I said I would take a news fast. I succeeded to a certain point but couldn't go the whole way. The news crept in here and there through conversations, through Facebook posts, through just going to the grocery store and looking over at the newspaper as I walked out. It was impossible to remove myself from the world.

However, I think I missed something that is now coming into view. I can be *"in the world but not of the world,"* as the Master teacher, Jesus, once said. In fact, in Reality, none of us are of this world. We are Spirit incarnated here, visiting here, and will at some point move on.

What is the best I can do while I am here? I do not think it is spending my time focused on the things that are happening in the world that I can never change. No, the best I can make of my time here is to be all I can be. I think I have to go back to focusing on my life of creativity, my goals, aspirations, and the dreams I still have to live. If I do not, I've become a prisoner. I am not a prisoner. I am free to choose. I am free to be. I am free to create. I am free to live the greatest life possible. My great life, in turn, reflects upon the world.

This is what has come to the top of my mind today as I sit in contemplation. I think I've become a little too distracted with things that are most likely prayer requests for me. I should do my Treatment work and let these troubles go to the Universal Law. As I go about my day, I will know if there is something I'm supposed to do.

Also, I remember, this world is my world and it is a reflection of my mind. Perhaps if I lift my mind higher through living more fully, the mirror will change also.

Affirmation:
I am in the world, but not of it.

95

Three = One

Have you ever compartmentalized your life? For example, it might be to pay bills or cook a meal or get well or do anything on the physical plane. You step into a mode of singular action. It can be stressful or easy, but still you are figuring things out or making ends meet on the physical plane. It seems that you are alone in a physical world.

Ernest Holmes once wrote about taking the Spirit into living. He was warning us not to separate the Spiritual from the physical. He wrote, "*We are one with the body of the physical world; One with the Creative Law of the Universe in the mental world; and One with the Spirit of God in the conscious world.*" Living in all three worlds at once is real living. "*...We shall expand, grow and express only to the degree that we consciously cooperate with the whole,*" he wrote.

I want to live this wholeness now. I know that it starts from the top—the *Spiritual*. If I can live from that place, Spirit's logic becomes my logic and thus becomes my *Mental* world. I think from a higher place. I don't have to figure things out because I know. The physical world then becomes an embodiment of the Spiritual and Mental. It just is. Everything out-pictures in perfection.

Challenges are not challenges anymore. They are opportunities to know more. They are opportunities to open up more—to unkink the hose of my thoughts and let more and more of the Spirit flow through by remembering that I am unlimited within the Universal.

I think that sometimes we get afraid to totally let go. We somehow think we will lose our individuality. This is not true. Our individualization or volition can never be removed from the equation. The day we learned we could think was the day we had the potential to realize who we were. We realized that we were free to choose. Choice is an attribute of Spirit. It equates with free Spirit.

So, today and every day, I will remind myself in every moment that I am living on three planes: *Spirit - Mind - Body*. I am one. I am living in wholeness. Behind every *Physical* aspect of my life, I know that the *Mental* world created it with my level of embodying *Spirit* in that moment.

If I want something in the *Physical* to change or expand, I must start at the top and be open to more of my true Identity in the *Spiritual* World and let it trickle down into my *Mental* world. I can do this in every aspect of my life. I am designing and redesigning my life in every moment.

Affirmation:
I am the designer of my life.

96

Get Out of J.A.I.L.

Did you ever feel like you were in jail? I have. I've had that feeling that I can't make a change, for example. I've felt trapped in a job or in a relationship or in a financial situation. I felt like something (outside of myself) was making it happen and there was nothing I could do about it.

Then I learned something amazing. I learned that I, and I alone, was responsible for my life. I learned that by changing my mind about something, I could change my circumstances.

One of the times that stands out in my mind was when I was in a job I wanted to leave. I wanted to go on to be a full-time minister. I had no job waiting for me and I felt that awful feeling of having to stay somewhere where I was unfulfilled. I needed to make a change, but I couldn't do it. I felt trapped and victimized by my situation. There was no change in the forecast. I finally got to the moment when I knew something had to give.

A dear friend and fellow ministerial student did a Spiritual Mind Treatment with me. The treatment wasn't for me leaving my job. He uncovered the lie which was that I felt that I was not free. The treatment was about freedom. I was free to choose whatever I wanted for my life. I do not remember the words of the Treatment. I only remember that in that moment, something within me changed and I felt supported and powerful and filled with the freedom of choice. It wasn't long after that the circumstances lined up and I became a full-time minister.

J.A.I.L. is just another word for *Just An Illusion created by Lies*. The Lies are numerous: the lie that we are choice-less; the lie that our future is dependent on our past; the lie that we are meant to be poor or sick or unhappy because of some karma. Lies, lies, lies, based in a belief in duality. There is only one Power and we are free to use it in any way we choose. The use of this Power is through the use of our minds. Ernest Holmes used to begin his talks with these words, *"There's a Power for Good in the Universe greater than we are and we can use it."*

If we want to get out of our self-imposed prisons, then we must begin right where we are and learn to use our minds on purpose. We must retrain ourselves to think with love for ourselves and for others. We must fill our minds with beauty, joy, and true wisdom.

Spiritual Mind Treatment changes things by revealing the Truth to us. It does this because there is a Law that responds to the impress of our thoughts and beliefs. Spiritual Mind Treatment changes our beliefs. It is not superstitious, mysterious, or a cult experience. It is not something that someone can do to us. It is the Power of the Word moving into Law. When we are receptive, like I was that day with my friend's treatment, we get into the flow of Good and begin attracting what we desire instead of the opposite. Our subconscious mind stops contradicting our conscious words. Spiritual Mind Treatment changes the lie we've been thinking to the Truth.

Affirmation:
My conscious mind and my subconscious mind are aligned for my good.

97

Everything Changed!

Have you ever felt like nothing changed but everything changed in a particular moment? I had that experience this week. I was struggling a bit financially, but only because I was looking at what was in our account. I kept looking to the outside and wondering how the necessary amount of finances would make themselves known so the dilemma could be solved. I kept looking out to past sources of income. I wondered if this or that would happen this month.

The more I looked out and tried to figure it out, the worse my state of mind got. I just couldn't fathom how the dilemma would be solved. Then, after realizing that I was doing exactly the opposite of what I say I believe, I spent lots of time within, in meditation and Treatment. I stopped looking out. I stopped trying to figure it out. I simply gave over; surrendered my dilemma to the Greater Mind. I stopped looking at it like a dilemma. It was only an experience.

My inner voice said, *"This is no big deal. I've been here before. I got myself here by thinking about this all month. Now, it is time to release it and stop worrying."*

Turning my fear to faith, I just let it all go. Nothing changed in the world of form, but something changed within me. That something was the security and peace of mind that comes from knowing that there is something greater than all of this that is holding me and caring for me. One of my mentors sent me a quote that struck me deeply.

"As I have told you before, I have not abdicated My Throne. Let this be your assurance. On this premise can you base you

calmness and quietness.... I created man and gave him the power to function in physical form. I allowed him to choose between good and evil, but I still hold all things in the hollow of My hand. ...My kingdom shall rule forever more, a kingdom based on love, trust and honesty. It must needs be born out of struggle and strife, for mortal thought will not give way easily, but born it shall be..."
Anonymous.

Although this quote is somewhat dualistic and I do not believe in an outside God, I do believe in the one Power, the Divine Presence that permeates all existence and lives through each of us. I do believe we get to choose between good and evil in every moment; evil, meaning thoughts that are fearful and negate life. I do feel that mortal thought tends not to give way easily. We might be born with a stubborn streak in us. We've come here to get over that stubborn streak and give over to Life itself that has never *"abdicated its throne"* and always holds us in the hollow of Its hand.

Well, my week continued and in an instant, although nothing on the outside had changed, everything changed. I became calm, peaceful, knowing. Then, as if it were a miracle, the floodgates of my life opened to match that calm. I'm just fine. I'll always be fine. Sometimes, I slide off my high horse. The good thing is I always know how to get back on. Spiritual Mind Treatment works, my friends, because it changes our consciousness.

I wonder sometimes if I will always have these little slip-ups. I don't know the answer to that. I just know that right now, in this present moment, all is well. If I had to work on anything, I would work on staying present because, in reality, in the present everything is taken care of for all of us.

Affirmation:
All is well in my world just as it is.

98

Is Your Oxygen Mask On?

When I say my life is unfolding perfectly it doesn't mean it is just because everything seems to be going smoothly. My life must always be unfolding perfectly, or not at all.

The more we can envision life the way we want to experience it and give gratitude for it, the more we will experience it that way. And, when things occur that are challenging or tragic, it is how we react to them that makes the difference.

If we really believed in the process of involution and evolution and used it on point, we would experience more of those things that we want to experience. What is involution and evolution? Simply put, involution is the contemplation of an idea in mind. It is the focusing of thought on a certain thing. Ernest Holmes writes, "*When we are dealing with Causation, we are dealing with that which has involved within Itself all effect, as it unfolds.*" This is the way that we demonstrate whatever we are demonstrating. All is thought, and of course, our thoughts come from our beliefs. We think as we have been taught to believe.

When something is not working in my life, I do not run for the hills or bury the feelings I am having. I do not say that I am not sad. I do not deny that I am not able to pay my bills. I do not deny a stomach ache. However, what I do is that I realize that this is not a necessity, and I trust the Law of my Being to bring me new results, as I go back to First Cause and really know the Truth about myself. Sometimes this is a process, and sometimes it is an instantaneous healing. It doesn't matter how long it takes. What matters is consistency. What matters is creating a mental atmosphere for myself that is focused on the joy of living.

In these challenging times where it is sometimes hard to see what good is unfolding, it is more important than ever to stay in the Light. We offer so much to the world by our own positive attitude and celebration of life. We will not bring more joy to the world if we suffer just because we see suffering in the world.

Last night we were with a group of friends enjoying an evening. As I looked around and saw everyone laughing from the depths of their being, I couldn't help but think that we have lifted the consciousness of the world in that moment. Why? Because we are all living in one Mind and what is felt by one is felt by all.

We can provide a rope of life to those suffering by expressing our joy. We can reach out with more power from a strong, joyful, and passionate consciousness than we can by wallowing in grief. This doesn't mean we are not compassionate or empathetic toward suffering. It just means while we are holding the fallen, we come from a state of Light and Love. It makes a difference. I have seen a person's whole demeanor and feelings change just by sitting with them in that state.

We are all beacons of Light. How much of our Light will we live, and therefore share, is the only question. Let it shine, shine, shine. And, remember, the one thing they tell you when you are taking off in a plane is if the oxygen masks drop due to a loss in pressure, please put your mask on first before trying to assist someone else.

Affirmation:
I take care of my own consciousness first and the consciousness of the world expands.

99

What's My Purpose?

As I reflect on the last two nights and everything that led up to it, I can feel what Spirit can do through us when we let go. I am speaking of the Cabaret evening that was the birthday fundraiser for Center for Spiritual Living Kaua`i.

At one time, singing and acting was all I wanted for my life. I worked so hard to bring my voice to a level of professionalism. I studied, sacrificed time and money, auditioned, performed, and had a level of success in a small pond. That's what they say, anyway. Is there anything really that is a small pond? I find that derogatory to those of us who bring joy to thousands in the community theater world. The two nights of Cabaret cannot be measured by or compared to Broadway in the level of influence on this planet. When a soul is touched and moved by something, the work has been worth it and the ripple effect of love travels out into the Universe.

So, after many years of not performing, I put myself up in the public eye last night. I overcame my insecurities and feelings that I might not have that great of a voice after all. I did it anyway. I remember there were times when I just gave it over to the Spirit. Interestingly, I felt that Spirit of my confidence in the form of my father who loved my voice. I felt like he was with me through this one, applauding me on.

Am I still a performer? It is an interesting question and when I ask it, I think no. Am I still a singer? It is one of the ways that I express myself that cannot be denied. However, it is not as it used to be. I have moved on from the deep yearning to be in show business. If I sing at all, it is to just give a part of myself that people seem to enjoy.

What am I now? Where am I going? What is mine to do and be? If I ask the question deeply, I feel that I am here to awaken others to their magnificence by being all I can be. Wherever that takes me, I am open to that. This ministry of love I have chosen has many facets, from bookkeeping to praying to speaking to singing to teaching to cleaning the floor after it's all over. Minister is a verb and when you live it from that point of view, you welcome opportunities to serve where you are called.

I am grateful that there was a time in my life where singing was my whole life and that I was able to bring that memory here to Kaua`i the last two nights and inspire and give some joy. We said our purpose was to bring more love to the planet. I think we accomplished that. If there was a note that wasn't quite there or a missed word, it is of little significance to the joy I saw in the eyes of a 91-year old woman who had her dream of beginning her life yet again affirmed through the experience of being at our Cabaret.

In everything that we strive to do in life, the purpose is fulfilled when we know we have expressed ourselves authentically and with complete surrender - when we have not been focused on the details of making sure we look good, but instead, the act of giving what we have to give. The creative process is an eternal expression of the One Power living and having Its way with each and every one of us. We are all part of that tapestry. Life is, and Life is a Cabaret sometimes.

Affirmation:
I surrender to my greatest self. I live my purpose.

100

Perfect Inaction

One thing that I have learned as we grow Center for Spiritual Living Kaua`i is what it means to be in perfect inaction. This is not something that can be taught. It can only be experienced. At one time, I didn't really understand it. I tried to grasp its meaning, but it wasn't until I started practicing it that the feeling began to overcome me. Perfect inaction doesn't mean we don't take action, it means that our minds are stayed in truth as we take appropriate, guided action. It means that we are not swayed to and fro with doubt and fear. We just know all is well.

We are ready to celebrate three years on the island of Kaua`i, and I believe it is perfect inaction that brought us to this point. The growth of Center for Spiritual Living Kaua`i has been a process of planting seeds of faith and expecting them to sprout. In fact, not even expecting them to sprout, but knowing that they have already sprouted. Each step in these three years has been taken in the unseen world and then backed up by action in perfect inaction. There has been no fretting, and when worry does come up, it is abolished with truth as quickly as possible.

Perfect inaction means a calm, peace-filled knowing that all is well. When we move with perfect inaction we are not flustered or disturbed by appearances. We simply know that everything is unfolding perfectly. It comes from the depths of one's soul as he/she sits in quiet contemplation of life. It comes from moving with something that comes from the depths of our passion and love. It comes by practicing faith and surrendering everything to the Law of our Being. It comes in the present moment and nowhere else.

As we enter our fourth year here on Kaua`i, I let go to continue in perfect inaction. I know that every step we take is guided and that each step is the perfect step right now. The next one taken will come in the right time. When something feels forced or like it's not working out, I know that I have stepped in the way. I've wanted it "my way," meaning my small ego mind that doesn't see the whole picture.

There is nothing that can be more powerful than perfect inaction. It is that knowing that is spoken of when we say "When you pray believe that you have it...and you will have it." What peace of mind comes with perfect inaction.

Affirmation:
I live in perfect inaction.

101

Health Maintenance Program

> "THE SUBSTANCE OUT OF WHICH MY BODY IS
> CREATED IS SPIRITUAL, AND IS MAINTAINED BY THE
> ALL-POWERFUL ESSENCE OF SPIRIT."
>
> ERNEST HOLMES

What a life-giving affirmation this is! Just try it on. I read it this morning and then used it in my prayer treatment. I have come to the realization that most of our physical problems are caused by our inability to turn our bodies over to the maintenance of the Spirit. We think we run the show with food, vitamins, exercise, and all of that, when in essence, it is the opposite.

Now, I am an advocate of all these things - food, vitamins, exercise, doctors, and the like. I partake in all of them, but not to the absence of Spirit. Spirit comes first and when I find myself lost in thinking that if I do a certain fad diet or a specific exercise that my physical issue will be erased, I know I am on the wrong track. Instead, if I start with the Spiritual, I am guided and led to the right physical practice.

Recently, I watched the film *Jonna's Body, Please Hold!* It is the true life story of a woman, Jonna, who experienced cancer and wrote a one-woman show about it. She personified every part of her body and her illness. Behind the scenes is the chief operator - her immune system - keeping everything together and flowing. At a crucial time, her immune system just gives up because it gets no help from Jonna.

The film has a powerful message. How often do we condemn everything about ourselves? We don't like the size of our breasts or other organs; we condemn our skin for its blemishes; we hate our weak muscles and wish our tummies were flatter. We even verbally attack ourselves by saying things like, "*I always get sick when...*" or "*I feel terrible!*"

We are hypnotized by media and current worldly beliefs to think that at certain ages this or that is going to happen. We actually believe it. Looking out into the world and into our lives we verify what we have believed every moment with every step. The media backs it all up with commercial upon commercial about every pill we can take to help us sleep, get skinnier, or resist the next flu epidemic. We are really stuck in the never-ending spiral of lack of ease in our bodies.

There is a way out and we cannot wait for ourselves to feel better before taking this road. The way to get to health is to claim it now. The way to get to health is to love ourselves well. I remember reading that the word incurable means "*not able to be cured.*" The root definition of cure is "*cared for.*" Why would we tell ourselves that we are not able to be cared for?

Spirit is all in all. It is running the show to the level of our acceptance and ability to turn ourselves over to it. We are perfect Spirit now, not at some future date. Can we accept wellness and vitality as our true nature or will we continue to be hypnotized into thinking we have to suffer? That is the question. I believe the best health maintenance program is self-care in the form of self-love and surrendering our bodies to the "*Spirit of Life.*"

Affirmation:
I live my life in self-care and self- love.

Epilogue

What is the Science of Mind?

The Science of Mind encompasses three things. Firstly, it is a philosophy because it includes the genius of the mystics and philosophers of all ages. If love is at the foundation of the philosophy, it is part of the Science of Mind.

Secondly, it is a religion, but not in the sense of having a dogma to which one must adhere. It shares the common thread with all other religions in the quest to know God. In the Science of Mind, one discovers God within one's self. As we know ourselves, we know God.

Thirdly, it is a science in that it teaches us to use the Laws of the Universe and to prove that these Laws work.

It is called the Science of Mind because we live in a mental Universe and the only way to use these Laws is with our mind, which is another word for Consciousness. There is one Mind in which we all reside, or as Ralph Waldo Emerson wrote, "*One Mind common to all individual men.*"

The Science of Mind is also a way of life because it is meant to be practiced and used. How else can we develop a philosophy, know God, and prove its principles?

Dr. Ernest Holmes, author, mystic, teacher, and the Founder of the organization called Religious Science and the Science of Mind philosophy once wrote, "*I would rather see a student of this Science prove its Principle than to have him repeat all the words of wisdom that have ever been uttered. It is far easier to teach the Truth than it is to practice it."*

So, what is its Principle and how is it practiced? It is simple. We are Spiritual Beings living in a Spiritual Universe, governed by our use of the Spiritual Law of Cause and Effect. I invite you not to try to make it more complicated by tearing at its simplicity. Instead, explore it, use it, and test it. If your life is better from an honest exploration and use of its Principle, then it is so worth the journey. At least it has been for me.

The Science of Mind is not about being positive. Yes, of course, we remain positive amidst life's challenges, but positivity without the substance of a deep understanding and real faith is superficial and not lasting. We can't just utter positive words without the belief to back them and expect to have a positive experience.

Ernest Holmes wrote, *"In the Science of Mind, we do not say everything is all right when it is all wrong. We do not say peace when there is no peace, but rather we try to discover what is wrong and why we do not have peace. We do not say that people are not poor, sick, or unhappy. We ask why these things should be if the Original Cause of all things is harmonious, perfect, radiant, and happy."*

What the Science of Mind isn't is a get-rich-quick plan. It takes faith, perseverance, and instances of failure to master its Principle. The rewards for those who persevere are great and include a life of true inner peace. This inner peace allows one to meet life's challenges with a deeper understanding and the ability to walk through those challenges.

The great discovery of the Science of Mind teaching is

that, even in the seeming failures we experience, we grow deeper into our True Selves. It is as if our Spirit is calling us home, calling us to go deeper, asking us to make a complete surrender to It, to trust It, and to rely on It completely.

As individuals, our ego sometimes holds on to its identification, no matter our suffering. The Science of Mind teaches that we will soon realize we have learned all we can through suffering. We are to have Joy! Yes, we shall overcome suffering at some point in our evolution.

I have suffered. I have watched others suffer. I have especially witnessed a world in suffering. I believe the time has come and we are ready to shift, to release what doesn't serve us, and to live in Unity.

The Science of Mind teaching challenges us to take 100% responsibility for our lives. We are always causing effect, and when we accept our Power and practice our complete faith in the Law of the Universe, we begin to respond differently to the relative world. Think of yourself as a vibration of energy magnetizing back to yourself a like vibration as your experience.

Ernest Holmes tells us, *"One of the most difficult problems to realize is that when we are dealing with the Law of Mind, we are dealing with an absolutely impersonal thing. …The ancients taught that there is an Infinite Self-Knowing Spirit and in addition to which there is an Infinite Law which knows how to do, but doesn't care what it does. This is the Karmic Law of Buddha, 'the Law that binds the ignorant and frees the wise.'"*

To truly practice the Science of Mind, one must be a humble student, willing to explore, willing to keep saying yes. One must have that Eye of the Tiger, which includes a clear vision of what we want and how we want to live. We have to be willing to walk that path no matter what appears to be in the way.

Having the "eye of the tiger" is an expression that refers to what the tiger's prey last sees prior to being killed. When the tiger goes in for the kill, it turns its ears backwards, showing the spot on the back of each ear, i.e., the "tiger's eyes."

If we practice the Science of Mind with the eye of the tiger, if we use the power of Spiritual Mind Treatment, those prey - negative beliefs – that separate us from recognizing our Divinity will at last perish. Stronger than a tiger's claws and teeth is the Power of Love. "*Love is a Cosmic Force whose sweep is irresistible,*" says Ernest Holmes.

The more we commune with Spirit through meditation, the more we train ourselves to turn away from the relative world and its effects, the greater our demonstrations will be. The practice of the Science of Mind assists its earnest students in changing their life by changing their energy. I know because I am one of those students and one of its teachers.

Acknowledgments

I am grateful to Dr. Ernest Holmes for his ability to see through the world of conditions to a higher consciousness and share that wisdom in a practical way with the world. The Science of Mind and Spirit has most definitely saved my life. I am also grateful for all the New Thought leaders that came before Dr. Holmes who had the courage to step outside of their belief systems to know a higher Truth.

I am grateful for the opportunity I had to raise three children, Jennifer, Kenneth, and Laura, who are all amazing individuals who bless the world in their own way. They inspire me every day.

I am grateful for my friend and proofreader, Sue Buckley, who dotted my i's and cross-checked every word I've written here.

I am grateful for my dear friend, Rev. Dr. Jonathan Zenz. He not only helped me to make sure this book got published. He is always there for me with Truth.

I am grateful to my CSL Kaua`i `Ohana. They teach me every single day how to be a better person and a better minister.

I am grateful to my mentor and friend, Dr. James Mellon, who has let me know in no uncertain terms that "I Am God." His mentoring and friendship have grown me into the minister I am today. And, I can't thank him without acknowledging his husband, Kevin Bailey and their two beautiful children, Nora and William.

I am grateful to the late Rev. Dr. Marlene Morris, my first minister in New Thought. She opened the door to my heart and to this Teaching. I would also like to acknowledge my very first Science of Mind teacher, Richard Morgan RScP, who challenged me to wake up to my calling as a Practitioner and Minister by recognizing and nurturing my True Identity.

And to the greatest of all, the man who introduced me to the Science of Mind in 1998 and who is my partner in spirituality, my lover, my husband, and my best friend, Patrick Feren. Meeting you, falling in love with you, and working side-by-side with you for over 24 years is the greatest gift of my life. I love you, Patrick!

About the Author

RITA ANDRIELLO-FEREN is an ordained Religious Science Minister, teacher, spiritual coach, writer, singer, and healer. She received her BA degree in Secondary Education and Communication and her MA in Theater and Directing from the University of New Mexico and has been immersed in New Thought spiritual studies and practice since 1998. Rita became a Practitioner and Minister at the NoHo Arts Center in Los Angeles, now known as Global Truth Center. She led the Outreach Prison Ministry and Pastoral Care Ministry at the Global Truth Center in addition to serving as Assistant Minister and Administrator to her Spiritual Director and mentor, Dr. James Mellon. Rita's background in the Arts includes a lifetime of writing, teaching, and developing spiritual and educational curriculum, as well as performance and vocal mastery. Her life's mission is to be a presence of Love to all. She is the Co-Spiritual Director of Center for Spiritual Living Kaua`i, a vibrant Science of Mind organization which she founded with her husband, Patrick Feren, in 2013. She is the mother of three and grandmother to five. Rita's first book *This Thing Called Treatment* is available on Amazon.

Made in United States
North Haven, CT
11 June 2022

20041358R00153